Vagus Nerve:

DISCOVER THE SECRETS TO UNLEASH YOUR NATURAL ABILITY TO OVERCOME ANXIETY, DEPRESSION, PTSD AND CHRONIC ILLNESS. A POLYVAGAL THEORY WITH STIMULATION EXERCISES.

Claire Watts

Table of Contents

Introduction 1

Chapter 1 What Is Vagus Nerve? 7

Chapter 2 Vagus Nerve Anatomy 20

Chapter 3 The Autonomic Nervous System 32

Chapter 4 Healing Benefits 40

Chapter 5 The Role Of The Vagus Nerve In Depression 53

Chapter 6 Other Functions 62

Chapter 7 What Is The Vagal Tone? 69

Chapter 8 Polyvagal Theory 79

Chapter 9 High Vagal Tone Vs. Low Vagal Tone 85

Chapter 10 The Relationship Of The Vagus Nerve With Other
Nerves And Conventional Medicine...........................91

Chapter 11 Vagus Nerve And Emotional Detachment 97

Chapter 12 Empathy, Socialization And Vagus Nerve 105

Chapter 13 Practical Self Help Exercises For Vagus
Nerve Activation 116

Chapter 14 Using Certain Equipment 128

Chapter 15 Chew and Whistle, A Medicinal Product That Can
Work In Cold And Common Breast Bronchitis 135

Chapter 16 Can Vagus Nerve Stimulation Treat
Heart Diseases? 139

Conclusion.. 148

Introduction

The vagus nerve acts as the regulator of the immune system. It indirectly is able to influence the immune system, changing the impacts of it. In particular, the vagus nerve is meant to activate when it detects cytokines, one of the chemicals associated with the immune system. These cytokines are meant to allow for communication between the various cells of the immune system and can cause the creation of even more inflammation.

The vagus nerve is meant to tell the cells in the body to stop producing the cytokines in general. It is usually activated in order to create anti-inflammatory responses throughout the body. Just as it does with the fight or flight response, the vagus nerve is meant to regulate the inflammatory response. This works to stop the immune system from overrunning itself. It is meant to be a sort of stop-gap to encourage the body to stop. When it fails, however, the immune system is able to run rampant. Inflammation throughout the whole body runs rampant and the individual suffering from the immune response is likely to have other struggles as well.

Usually, the vagus nerve struggles at doing its job like this when it is not toned. Without the necessary tone, the vagus nerve cannot activate and regulate regularly and effectively, and in response, you find that you are more likely to suffer from varying degrees of inflammation. However, you can also begin to regulate inflammation, lessening its effects by making sure that you strengthen and activate your vagus nerve.

It is responsible for regulating out the fight or flight response through the activation of the parasympathetic nervous system. This allows the body to begin to relax, overcoming all of those feelings and physical responses that lead to fear and anxiety in the first place.

However, sometimes, this does not work as expected. Sometimes, with constant low vagal activity, the body gets taken over by anxiety, so to speak. We are going to take a period of time to take a look in particular at anxiety disorders, anxiety, and the vagus nerve, and finally, the implications created about the vagus nerve.

Anxiety Disorders

Anxiety is suffered by a staggering estimated 40,000,000 in just the United States alone. This means that roughly 18% of the world is suffering from anxiety in some form or another. Despite this, only about 37% of people ever seek any sort of treatment to help them mitigate and control their anxiety. The rest simply let it run rampant without ever attempting to fix the problem.

When you suffer from anxiety, you are likely to find that you struggle immensely with regulating your emotions. It can come in many different forms, ranging from mild general anxiety all the way to extreme post-traumatic stress disorder, with many other possibilities between them. All of these different disorders share one thing in common: They are related to the vagus nerve. Before we delve into this, however, let's go over some of the most common anxiety symptoms that you can suffer from:

- You may feel irritable and nervous all of the time
- You feel like there is danger lurking somewhere and cannot find it
- Your heart rate is elevated
- You breathe rapidly
- You feel weak
- You struggle to concentrate
- You struggle to sleep
- You suffer from gastrointestinal issues

These symptoms can all layer together to create several disorders that are regularly classified together. Now, let's take a look at some of these anxiety disorders:

- Panic disorder: This is sudden extreme episodes of terror that strike completely at random. You do not know when to expect them, but when they hit, you find that you are suffering from heart palpitations and feel like you are going to die or that you are having a heart attack.

- Social anxiety disorder: This is also commonly referred to as a social phobia. When you have this, you are incredibly self-conscious to the point that you worry regularly about what people around you are going to think about you. You are fixated on how likely it is that other people are going to judge you and you feel embarrassed by it.

- Phobias: These are intense fears on specific stimuli that are usually quite irrational, and yet you cannot get past them. Despite knowing that they are irrational, you find that you cannot stop it from happening.

- Generalized anxiety disorder: This is an excessive, unrealistic worry that you cannot relieve. You are unsure why you are suffering from it, but it is there, underlying everything.

- Post-traumatic stress disorder: This is the result of trauma that was never properly processed. It manifests as sudden extreme terror, usually in relation to some sort of stimulus. It typically presents with flashbacks as well.

Anxiety And The Vagus Nerve

Anxiety and the vagus nerve go hand in hand. When you suffer from anxiety, your vagus nerve is not functioning properly. It is not activating when it should, and this means that your body is unable to turn off the negative responses that you are having. Your sympathetic nervous system remains active for far too long, leading to a buildup of cortisol and other stress-related hormones, and as a result of this, you begin to see the above disorders arising.

You need to activate your parasympathetic response if you hope to override that lack of vagus nerve involvement. In fact, this is something that you probably already do if you have been taught to use deep breathing or meditation and mindfulness in order to control your own anxiety. When you trigger your vagus nerve, your body goes through a response that discourages stress and anxiety. Instead of being anxious all of the time, you find that you are instead able to turn on that rest and digest mode. Instead of being terrified to be around other people, you are able to regulate yourself. You are able to keep yourself functioning properly, and that is what matters. You are able to correct yourself and ensure that you do respond to the stress in a manner that is effective, and that is important.

Trauma, Post-Traumatic Stress Disorders, and the Vagus Nerve

Trauma experienced in your life also changes your body's chemistry, much like how the activation of anxiety does. When you suffer from trauma, your body goes into that fight or flight response—your body is preparing to defend itself by fighting off the threat, but it may also have to act by running away. It prepares for this by directing blood to the extremities, giving the muscles the boost that they would need. It also makes sure that the heart is pumping and running quicker so more oxygen can be pumped throughout the body.

For most of us, when the trauma ends, we return to that parasympathetic rest and digest mode. However, for some people, you find that you remain in the sympathetic fight or flight mode. Instead of being able to relax, you find that you continue to be on high alert for any sort of threat that could potentially lead to problems for you. In turning on this fight or flight response, your body continues to relive the trauma. You are tense, you are nervous, and you feel like the trauma never ended—because to your body, it never did. Your body continues to treat it like it is suffering, and you do not recover the way most would. This leads to the creation of PTSD.

When you are able to activate the vagus nerve, however, you will find that you can actually begin to tackle those feelings that otherwise would be problematic for you. You can begin to sort of kick-start your mind into activation. You can make sure that the mind is more likely to go along with what it needs to, all because you are able to activate it effectively. With a toned vagus nerve, then you would start to see relief from your PTSD symptoms as well. After all, when you cannot get out of that initial fight or flight response, you cannot begin to process or recover what has happened.

Chapter 1 What Is Vagus Nerve?

The name "vagus" is Latin for "wanderer". This means that the vagus nerve wanders and meanders throughout the body. It is a cranial nerve that runs throughout the entire body. It is associated to the parasympathetic nervous system (PNS). As such, it is the main highway by which the Central Nervous System (CNS) communicates with the PNS. As such, it is tremendously important in regulating all of the essential bodily functions that the PNS regulates.

Given the fact that it is so important, it is surprising just how overlooked this nerve actually is. In addition, we will be discussing how your understanding of this nerve can help you increase your overall health and wellness. So, sit tight because we are going to be discussing quite a bit of information here. You will surely find this to be insightful as well as fascinating.

We will begin by looking deep into two crucial components of the vagus nerve, the Pneumogastric Nerve and the Ventral Branch of the vagus nerve.

The Pneumogastric Nerve

Before modern research on the vagus nerve was conducted, the name it commonly received was the "pneumogastric nerve". It has earned this designation since the vagus nerve is responsible for the regulation of the heart, lungs and digestive tract.

As the pneumogastric nerve is responsible for ensuring the proper functioning of these systems through the PNS. The PNS relies on the pneumogastric nerve to relay the right information to and from the CNS and the brain. Yet, the fact that the pneumogastric nerve starts in the brain and works its way down into the lungs, heart and digestive tract, it essentially becomes one of the most important neural networks in the body. Needless to say, that if something goes haywire in the pneumogastric nerve, it can lead to serious consequences in the rest of the body.

The pneumogastric nerve begins in the brain and leaves through the medulla oblongata. Then, it basically runs straight through the middle of the body down the neck, chest and into the abdomen. The pneumogastric nerve has ramifications, or branches, that touch upon the main organ systems described earlier.

First, the pneumogastric nerve connects into the laryngeal nerve and then curves around the subclavian artery so that it emerges between the trachea and the esophagus. This is where it is able to regulate the functioning of the lungs. As such, this nerve enables the PNS to regulate breathing.

The nerve runs down from the subclavian artery into the superior vena cava. From there, it moves on onto the bronchus before settling into the vagal trunk that passes through the diaphragm. It also connects into the carotid artery in which then allows it to link with the cardiac tissue. This is the point at which the pneumogastric nerve enables the PNS to hook up with the heart.

As the pneumogastric nerve makes its way down the esophagus and through the diaphragm, it is now able to link up with the digestive tract. This is what permits the PNS to regulate digestion.

As you can see, the pneumogastric nerve is truly an intricate piece of hardware which enables the PNS to regulate some of the most complex bodily functions. Needless to say, the body would not be able to function adequately without the pneumogastric nerve.

The pneumogastric nerve has the following branches which serve as means of communication among the entire routing of this nerve:

•Anterior vagal trunk

•Branches to the esophageal plexus

•Branches to the pulmonary plexus

•Hering-Breuer reflex in alveoli

•Inferior cervical cardiac branch

•Pharyngeal nerve

•Posterior vagal trunk

•Recurrent laryngeal nerve

- Superior cervical cardiac branches of vagus nerve

- Superior laryngeal nerve

- Thoracic cardiac branches

These branches are what enables the pneumogastric job to do its job effectively. When the system is firing on all cylinders, the communication flows effortlessly and regulation happens without a hitch. However, when there is a disruption in communication, or if the pneumogastric nerve becomes altered in any fashion, disruptions may occur leading to any number of potential medical conditions. We will dig deeper into these conditions.

The Ventral Branch Of The Vagus Nerve

The emergence of Polyvagal Theory has allowed for a deeper understanding of the nervous system and its effects on the overall wellbeing of the body. Generally speaking, the vagus nerve is considered as one mega-unit which regulates a number of vital biological systems. We have covered this in-depth.

At this point, we can dive straight into the discussion of Porges' Polyvagal approach explains the effect of the vagus nerve on the body. Since the vagus nerve is at the forefront of the PNS, it has a calming effect on the SNS.

Let's elaborate on that point further.

For instance, a person has been involved in a minor car accident, a fender-bender if you will. The incident itself is rather stressful though it does not bear any major consequences. As such, the individual is just shaken up and in need of some rest in order to get over what has occurred. In this example, the SNS kicked into high gear at the occurrence of the accident since the brain perceived a potential threat, that being the car accident. After closer inspection, there were no injuries, and everything proved to be rather innocuous.

If the PNS did not exist, there would be no way for the SNS to essentially shut off; the individual would remain at a constant state of stress and anxiety. Needless to say, they would not be able to sleep or eat due to the stress on them. This harkens back to the point we made earlier about prolonged stress and the effect it has on the overall nervous system.

After the brain has perceived that the threat is over, the PNS takes over and begins to bring back bodily functions down to normal parameters. This means that pulse and heart rate return to normal, blood pressure decreases, and the metabolism resumes normal operations. In the theory, all is well, and the individual makes a full recovery after a good night's sleep.

As a corollary, it is important to highlight the fact that sleep is a great equalizer. This is why you tend to feel sleepy after a significant spike in stress. Sleep allows the PNS to regulate body functions and bring the entire system back to normal. If you are unable to sleep, then the lasting effects will take much longer to become subdued thereby leading you to feel as if you had been hit by a train.

Of course, the active part only springs into action when there is the need for it, while the passive role hums along in the background.

That being said, the Polyvagal theory suggests that there is a third component of the system. A component which Purges called the "social engagement" system. In a way, this is a smart system that requires the removal of any perceived threat. What this implies is that we need to be able to discern when there is a threat and when there is not. When this discrimination occurs, it is not the "passive" side that takes over, but rather, it is the social engagement side of the equation.

Main functions of the vagus nerve

The vagus nerve is one large highway that conducts the flow of information from the biological systems that it controls up to the CNS. This is the main of the vagus nerve. In a manner of speaking, the vagus nerve is like a central command post in which the information comes and goes. Consequently, the vagus nerve provides the CNS with all of the data it needs to keep the body alive.

Let's assume that the vagus nerve simply stops working for whatever reason. In such a situation, the person would simply die. How so? If the vagus nerve stops sending information to the CNS, the CNS may conclude that the heart and lungs have stopped functioning. Therefore, the brain may have no choice but to begin shutting down other organ systems as well. This type of response may lead doctors to place a patient on life support.

This example highlights the importance that the vagus nerve has on the body's overall ability to sustain life. Now, let's assume that the vagus nerve is functioning properly, but there is some kind of damage to one of the organ systems. In that case, the vagus nerve relays the data on the damage to the organ system backup to the CNS. The brain then sends back the information through the vagus nerve and adjusts accordingly. For instance, if one lung is severely damaged, the brain may choose to shut down that lung and shift all of the breathing functions to the other healthy lung. This is enough to keep the body alive though not necessarily at peak performance.

In addition, the vagus nerve is the main command post for the digestive system. This is a crucial function to consider since the digestive system provides the body with the nutrition it needs to repair itself, fuel movement and keep cells running along. Hence, the digestive system needs close attention. This causal link between the digestive system and the CNS explains why folks who have undergone a traumatic experience often experience digestive distress. When the nervous system suffers a significant jolt, it is not uncommon to see that it has serious repercussions on the entire network controlled by the vagus nerve.

So, let's move on and take a deeper look at the specific functions that are associated with the vagus nerve.

The Visceral Somatic Function

Given the fact that the vagus nerve is part of the Autonomic Nervous System (ANS), it is inextricably linked to the entire body. Think of it as a main highway that receives traffic from all over the region even if the majority of motorists don't actually plan to stay in that particular area. In a way, the main traffic is just passing through.

Based on that premise, any disruption in the flow of traffic in that area may lead to disruption in the flow of traffic in other seemingly unrelated areas. The same goes for the nervous system and biological functions.

When we refer to a somatic function, we are talking about the reaction that comes as a result of the stimuli in the environment surrounding an organism. In this case, the human body is the organism immersed in a given environment.

As such, the somatic function that the vagus nerve plays is one of constant monitoring and regulation. Think of it as one large pressure valve that looks to regulate the build-up within a large engine. If too much pressure builds up, then the engine may explode. The same goes for the nervous system.

With that in mind, there is one interesting bit of good news... if we could call it that. The body is adept at adjusting to its environment. So, if the individual finds themselves consistently inundated by stressful situations, there is the possibility that the body will become adjusted to such levels of stress. In a way, it creates a "new normal".

An example of this attitude can be seen in the so-called "adrenaline junkies". These people become addicted to extreme sports due to the exhilaration that they get from engaging in a dangerous activity. However, they consistently need to up the ante since their nervous system constantly adjusts to the level of danger in each activity. So, in order to get the same rush, they need to overload their nervous system more and more. Otherwise, they may not find the same amount of enjoyment in the same activities.

As far as the visceral function is concerned, the vagus nerve is constantly tracking the performance of the body's internal organ systems. As a matter of fact, it is designed with a number of automatic switches that are intended to protect the body from grievous damage. Think of these switches like circuit breakers in an electrical system. When the system is overloaded by the electrical current, the circuit breaker is tripped thereby protecting the entire system. If no such breaker existed, the wiring would overheat potentially causing a fire.

The vagus nerve has built-in parameters that prevent the body from overexerting itself to the point where permanent damage is done to organs. Consider this situation:

A person who has been working non-stop for a week may find that after going on little to no sleep, they simply crash and sleep for an extended period of time. This reaction is triggered in the nervous system in order to prevent the heart from literally burning out. This is why drug consumption, the kind that disrupts the nervous system, making it prone for individuals to suffer from cardiac arrest. Since the substance wreaks havoc with the PNS natural regulation mechanisms, the body keeps going until it eventually shuts down.

A good example of this can be seen in modern cars. The car's computer shuts the engine down when it diagnoses a potentially serious problem in the engine. The car's control computer module shuts off the flow of gas, for example, in order to keep the engine from completely failing. The car will restart once the issue has been corrected.

So, just like a car's control module, the vagus nerve serves as the body's main regulation unit. This protects the body's vital organs from failing altogether at which point death would ensue. This is why optimal performance from the vagus nerve is essential to ensuring the body's overall optimal performance.

The Physical Motor Function Since the vagus nerve is part of the overall ANS, it is also connected to the body's peripheral nervous system which controls the movement of limbs. As such, the vagus nerve is involved in the motor functions of the body.

Now, the vagus nerve itself does not regulate movement, but it does regulate the biological functions that aid movement. The following example will illustrate this point.

When a person engages in physical activity, the CNS broadcasts the necessary signals to the limbs for movement, be it running, swimming, and so on. However, the heart is also responsible for supplying blood to the muscles while the lungs need to provide oxygen. Furthermore, there is an increased metabolic response as the body needs to create the energy it requires to sustain the level of physical activity. If the activity exceeds the heart's capacity to pump blood and the lungs' ability to provide oxygen, then the individual may simply get tired and stop moving.

This example highlights how important the vagus nerve is when taking movement into account. High-performance athletes have trained not only for their sport, but also develop stamina. Now, you may have heard of this term, yet it is generally associated to endurance, that is, sustaining physical activity over longer periods of time. But the fact of the matter is that stamina is the body's ability to provide the elements the body needs to sustain prolonged periods of physical activity.

Consequently, the vagus nerve is able to recognize these increased levels of physical activity and make the necessary adjustments so that muscles get the elements they need in order to keep going. It should be noted that the vagus nerve will also recognize when an athlete is becoming overexerted. At which point, the athlete may feel like they can't go on anymore. This is the body's protective measures that keep it from causing serious damage.

This last point illustrates the importance of keeping a balanced nervous system so that the vagus nerve can perform its functions appropriately thereby allowing the body's organ systems to provide the elements that the body requires.

Essential biological functions

These functions are what basically keeps the body alive. After all, if your heart stops breathing, then chances are you are not going to make it.

With that in mind, it is important to note that when the vagus nerve is not functioning at 100%, that is, when there is some kind of disruption, the essential biological systems may begin to go haywire. In some cases, it might be a slow and progressive disruption while in other cases it may be a sudden and shocking disruption.

Let's consider two possible scenarios:

An individual who has been working a stressful job begins to feel the effects of chronic stress over months or even years of accumulated stress. Suddenly, they may develop cardiac conditions, anxiety or even chronic digestive disorders. Yet, the progression of these conditions was so subtle that the person didn't really feel much of a difference.

On the flip side, there is a person who underwent a major traumatic incident, for instance, the loss of a loved one. The stress caused by the sudden loss of a dear person may cause a sudden overload to the nervous system. This sudden overload may lead to the onset of any of the aforementioned conditions. This may prompt swift intervention by medical professionals in order to address the onset of the symptoms the person is experiencing.

Chapter 2 Vagus Nerve Anatomy

The nervous system helps the different parts of the body to communicate with each other. It allows the body's systems to respond to changes and stimuli both within and outside our body. The entire system is truly a marvel of our body's engineering, able to coordinate various actions, responses, and functions. But it does not do this alone. In fact, the nervous system is itself a compilation of various smaller structures.

You could think of it like a large global corporation. From the outside, we can look at the corporation and admire it for its efficiency and success. But we all know that the organization is only successful because of the many smaller moving parts inside, namely, the staff, management, laborers, specialists, and leaders. Without them, the organization is a husk, incapable of doing anything on its own.

Among the many components of the nervous system, we have the cranial nerves, part of the peripheral nervous system. There are 12 pairs of cranial nerves.

What Are Cranial Nerves?

The cranial nerves refer to those nerves that come out directly from the brain. They are different from other kinds of nerves, such as spinal nerves that emerge from the spinal cord. Since the brain is the origin point for the cranial nerves, they are responsible for transferring information from the brain to various parts of the body, mostly to and from different parts of the neck and head.

One of the more unique features of the cranial nerves is that each one is paired and they are present on both sides of the body or the brain.

You have 12 pairs of cranial nerves and we are going to go through all of them so you can see just how important each of these nerves is.

- Olfactory nerve: Focused on smell so you can inhale the wonderful scents of that Fettuccine Alfredo that you prepared earlier

- Optic nerve: Responsible for transferring information from the retina to the brain, allowing you to see the beauty of the world around you or enjoy Avengers: Infinity War in the local cinema

- Oculomotor nerve: Controls the movement of the eye, the opening of the eyelid, and the constriction of the pupil

- Trochlear nerve: This nerve is responsible for innervating the oblique muscle of the eye. By doing so, it controls the rotational movement of your eyes.

- Trigeminal nerve: Handles the motor and sensory functions in the mouth and the face; ever enjoyed the wonderful feeling of a cool breeze on your face? You can thank the trigeminal nerve for that.

- Abducens nerve: This nerve is responsible for innervating the eye's lateral rectus muscle. As the name of the muscle suggests, the nerve controls lateral movement.

- Facial nerve: How do you look when you are sad, angry, happy, disgusted, afraid, or express the many human emotions you have? All of these facial expressions are controlled by the facial nerve, which is also responsible for the sensation of taste from the anterior parts of the tongue to the oral cavity.

- Vestibulocochlear nerve: This nerve is attached to the inner ear and is responsible for transferring information about sound and equilibrium to the brain from the inner ear.

- Glossopharyngeal nerve: Responsible for sending information from the middle ear, the pharynx, the tonsils, and the tongue

- Vagus nerve: Responsible for numerous tasks, some of which include sweating, heart rate, muscle movement in the tongue (including movements made for speech), keeping the larynx open for the purpose of breathing, and gastrointestinal peristalsis (which is a series of movements used for moving food in the body)

- Spinal accessory nerve: Certain functions of the neck and shoulder are controlled by this nerve.

- Hypoglossal nerve: Swallowing, speech, and food manipulation are the functions that are controlled by this nerve.

The above list gives you a gist of what each nerve is responsible for. But to get a deeper understanding of them, let us look at each nerve and see how they sometimes manage numerous functions at the same time.

Olfactory Nerve

As we saw in the list provided above, this nerve is responsible for the sense of smell. Of the 12 cranial nerves, the olfactory nerve is the shortest one. It is also one of the two nerves that have no connection to the brainstem, with the optic nerve being the other one.

Many other nerves possess two trunk-like protrusions. But the olfactory nerve is devoid of such a feature. Rather, it possesses fibers that go through the cribriform plate of the ethmoid bone, which is the part of the skull that is situated behind the nose. Essentially, these fibers of the olfactory nerve are also called neural receptors. When particles or chemicals in the air pass through the nose, they interact with these receptors. The molecules of these particles or chemicals stimulate the receptors and the message is then transferred to the brain. The brain, in turn, recognizes the message and lets you know what you are smelling. Do you want to know the most incredible part of all of these steps? All of this happens within just a fraction of a second. The part from the entrance of the molecules to your nasal cavity to the recognition of the scent is all so fluid and quick that you won't even know if the process has happened until you begin to recognize the scents.

Optic Nerve

Welcome to the visual world.

Do you like watching Game of Thrones? Do you enjoy reading? Do you love traveling around the world and witnessing the beauty of things? Well, don't forget to thank your optic nerve for its hard work.

You can find the optic nerve at the back of the eye. It is also the second cranial nerve. This nerve contains over one million nerve fibers and is made of nerve cells. All of these fibers and cells help process visual information.

All of us have what is called the "blind spot" in our eye. This is caused in the region where the optic nerve enters the eye, where there is an absence of special light-sensitive cells known as photoreceptors.

Oculomotor Nerve

Blinking is such a natural part of the human process that we hardly pay attention to it. The average person blinks about 15-20 times per minute. But how many of those blinks are we actually aware of? In fact, now that I mentioned blinking, you are probably more aware of your blinks (and you just want to stop being aware because it is not fun thinking about each and every blink that occurs). The oculomotor nerve is responsible for the movement of the eyelids, allowing you to perform your blinks naturally.

Additionally, the nerve also controls the movement of your eyeball. It controls those muscles in the eye that are used for visual tracking. When something moves across your field of vision, then your eyes become fixed on it because of the oculomotor nerve. If you have seen any of the James Bond movies, then you know how the superspy follows a person across the room using only his eyes and without moving his head? Well, if Bond's oculomotor nerve decided not to function normally, then he might just have to rotate his entire head to look at his target, making him the most obvious spy on the planet.

Trochlear Nerve

This nerve is the only one among the cranial nerves that appears near the back of the brain. While the oculomotor nerve is responsible for the overall movement of the eyes, the trochlear nerve manages the up and down movement of the eyes.

You might think that the trochlear nerve does not have such a big responsibility as compared to the other cranial nerves. But one must realize that any damage to the trochlear nerve results in double vision. This prevents us from walking properly, especially when we are using stairs. As the nerve focuses on up and down movement, we might have difficulty properly focusing on our movement on elevated surfaces (as we need to look both up and down to maintain balance and direction).

Trigeminal Nerve

This nerve gets to boast about being the largest of the cranial nerves. We use these nerves to transmit sensory information to the sinuses, skin, and the mucous membranes spread around our faces. For example, if you wanted to clench your jaw because you were angry or frustrated, then the trigeminal nerve is responsible for giving you the ability to do so. It also facilitates the movement of the jaw muscles.

Here are the parts of the body that information is transmitted to:

- Upper parts of the sinuses
- Cornea of the eye
- Chin
- Upper eyelid and associated mucous membranes
- Lower part of the mouth and the associated mucous membranes
- Front and middle parts of the tongue
- Lower lip
- Scalp
- Bridge of the nose
- Forehead
- Outer part of the ear
- Teeth of the lower jaw and the associated mucous membranes

Abducens Nerve

Are you able to move your eyes sideways? Are you able to move them away from the nose? Some people have the talent to focus both their eyes on the nose in a cross-eyed face, allowing many children to giggle at the ability. All of these movements of the eye are controlled by the abducens nerve.

One might think that the abducens nerve is responsible for so little compared to other nerves. But damage to the nerve means that you might maintain crossed eyes permanently. If not crossed eyes per se, then your eyes won't be aligned properly.

Facial Nerve

You put the keys into the lock of your apartment's main door. You turn the key and open the door, entering your apartment. The light switch is on your right and you flip it on. And suddenly, you see your friends and family in your apartment, who immediately shout, "Happy birthday!"

You are genuinely surprised and it shows on your face. But the nerve that is responsible for displaying the emotion is your facial nerve. Without it, you would look like an expressionless zombie and your friends and family would be left wondering just what they did wrong. But apart from determining your facial expressions, the nerve also has a small role to play in the sensory information in the tongue.

Most of the problems that occur in the facial nerve project themselves in the form of facial paralysis, where you are unable to control the muscles of a part or the entirety of your face. These problems can either be viral in nature or caused by certain genetic factors.

Vestibulocochlear Nerve

The vestibulocochlear nerve is also commonly known by another name, the auditory nerve. It is situated in the auditory canal of the ears.

When you enjoy your favorite music, listen to what people have to say in a conversation, or maybe even enjoy the sounds of nature, then you owe it to the vestibulocochlear nerve for making it all possible. Not only is the nerve responsible for hearing, but it also helps you with equilibrium.

"But, author," you say. "How can this nerve influence equilibrium?"

That is a good question indeed.

You see, we maintain balance by taking information from various sensory organs. This allows the body to measure its presence in relation to the ground and gravity. The signals received by the vestibulocochlear nerve is one piece of information that the brain receives in order to maintain balance. The brain receives these signals and sends information to the rest of the body to maintain posture and balance. If there are any abnormalities in the signals because of the way we are walking or the ground beneath us, then that information is received by the brain and it corrects our body's posture and arranges our limbs to regain our sense of balance.

Any damage received to the vestibulocochlear nerve causes sensations of vertigo, which also causes us to move haphazardly.

Glossopharyngeal Nerve

The glossopharyngeal nerve is arranged in such a way that it links to the brainstem, which is located in the upper medulla. It also runs through the base of the skill and finally connects to the tonsils, the base of the tongue and the glands in the mouth. This allows it to remain in control of various essential functions in the mouth.

For example, try saying this out loud: "I enjoy chocolate cake."

Try and hear the way you said it. Listen to the tone or pitch of your voice. Pay attention to how you sounded when you spoke those words. All of this is possible because of the glossopharyngeal nerve. This is because this nerve is responsible for the lingual and communication capabilities, but it does not work alone. In fact, it connects to the vagus nerve and together, they share the lingual and communication responsibilities in your mouth.

The nerve also plays an important role in the digestive process (that is made using the saliva) and also helps the body with rest.

Vagus Nerve

The vagus nerve is an important nerve that has numerous features. However, for now, let us look at some of the features of this nerve.

The vagus nerve is the longest nerve that is part of the cranial structure. It begins at the brain stem and from there, extends all the way to the colon. It is for this reason that the vagus nerve has numerous features. For example, it can actually stimulate the muscles in the heart, making it an important nerve in the regulation of heart rate. It also helps the body to move the body through the digestive tracts, from the esophagus to the stomach and beyond.

And as we have seen, it combines with the glossopharyngeal nerve for the purpose of communication and speech. In fact, if there is damage to the vagus nerve, then one of the problems faced by people is a complete loss of voice or difficulty in speaking. And because the vagus nerve is such an important component in the larynx, people might also have difficulty swallowing fluids when this nerve is damaged.

Spinal Accessory Nerve

Rotate your head around your neck. Now tilt your head to the side (any side will do). Tilt it to the opposite side. Nod your head.

Were you able to perform all of the above actions without any problems? Well, congratulations, your spinal accessory nerve is functioning really well. However, if you experienced any discomfort or pain while you were moving your neck, then it is not just because of the spinal accessory nerve. There could be a whole lot of reasons. If that happens, make sure you check in with a doctor.

Having said that, it is not just the neck that the spinal accessory nerve regulates. The nerve is also responsible for the smooth functioning of the shoulder and upper back. Have you ever seen the way ballet dancers adjust their shoulders when they stretch their arms or their upper back posture as they rotate on their toes? The ability to control such adjustments and postures is possible because of the work done by the vagus nerve.

Hypoglossal Nerve

The hypoglossal is the final nerve in the cranial nerve arrangement. This nerve starts its journey from the brainstem and then goes all the way to the tongue, connecting to the jugular and the carotid artery on the way.

The hypoglossal helps control the movement and prevent the paralysis of the tongue. If there was a problem with the nerve, then the patient would be asked to stick out the tongue, which would then point towards the direction of the paralyzed side. For example, if paralysis has occurred on the right side, then the tongue would point towards that side. If the hypoglossal nerve is permanently damaged, then the tongue would suffer more complications such as shrinking in size.

Chapter 3 The Autonomic Nervous System

The autonomic nervous system is a part of the nervous system that controls bodily functions that we are not consciously aware of controlling. In order for us to understand the autonomic nervous system, we need to know that the nervous system is made up of two opposing systems that are constantly sending information back and forth the brain and back to the organs.

The sympathetic side of the autonomic nervous system is mostly in control of your energy levels, alertness during the course of the day, your blood pressure, breathing, and heart rate.

This part of the system prepares us to act when it is needed and greatly affects hormones that give you your fight or flight reactions, namely adrenaline and cortisol levels. The parasympathetic side of the nervous system which contains most of the vagus nerve's functions and which the vagus nerve is greatly a part of, is there to decrease alertness, help with calming effects on the body, lower your heart rate and blood pressure, as well as aid your body with relaxation in stressful moments and help with digestion. Because the vagus nerve is a large part of the parasympathetic system, it also plays a role in helping with urination and defecation as well as sparking sexual arousal!

You can picture these two systems working together much like the accelerator and brake in a car.

The sympathetic nervous system would be your accelerator and it gets us up and going with all the energy in the world, and then when it comes time to calm down and relax, the parasympathetic nervous system will be your decelerator and will therefore reduce the speed at which we are going, and will then use certain neurotransmitters such as acetylcholine in order to lower your blood pressure and heart rate and cause the organs of the body to slow down their processes, too.

How To Activate Vagus Nerve?

Around 1921, a physiologist of Germany named Otto Loewi found out that by stimulating —what he called in German, vagusstoff —one can reduce the heart rate. Thus, the first ever neurotransmitter, acetylcholine was discovered which proved to be very helpful in dealing with a plethora of health problems, be it the mental or the physical problems.

The vagus nerve, once stimulated, can cause a wide variety of benefits, both the physical and the mental benefits since it elicits the relaxation response. The activation of the vagus nerve causes your sympathetic nervous system to release cortisol —and other hormones that are suitable for the situation —and it also helps to keep your immune system going all well and healthy for a short time period. It also triggers the long-term stress suppressing immunity and prepares us for emergencies (The fight or flight response), the key to unlock it is to activate it. And how do you do that? Follow the instructions below, these are some ways you can stimulate your vagus nerve:

33

1. Breathing techniques: As suggested by many authors and health experts, deep breathing helps people combat fearful, intense situations by energizing the vagus nerve but there are various techniques and breathing techniques that help stimulate the vagus nerve quickly.

- Intent fully long and slow belly breaths as you make a little time for yourself and allow yourself to be relaxed and at peace.

- Coherence or resonance breathing where people breathe gradually between five to seven times per minute.

- Conscious breathing for 10 to 15 minutes per day and increasing the time on daily basis.

2. Diving reflex or using any cold stimulus: You can just wash your face with cold water and activate your vagus nerve in no time. Also, you can use icepacks all over your face and get rid of your anxiety, depression, increased heart rate and many other benefits.

3. Singing and Chanting: This refers to using different mantras that calms the heart and relaxes the body whereas singing improves the heartbeat causing self-regulation through the stimulated vagus nerve. People also root for humming because it is reported to influence the nervous system state.

4. Joyful smile and a hearty laugh: Smiling more also stimulates the vagus nerve. This causes the heart rate to be normalized quicker. The laughter helps the person prevent heart diseases since the vagus nerve is stimulated by that action.

5. Yoga: Yoga postures like Ujjayi pranayama, sarvangasana (yoga for joy and peace), vipareet karani mudra and halasana are much preferred and suggested by the experts to stimulate the vagus nerve.

6. Meditation: The practice of meditation or what people call zazen is also a very effective stimulus which easily activates the vagus nerve and achieve the desired state of the internal body system. Meditation increases the activity of the genes that causes the self-regulation to take place which is a very crucial activity. Some people in South Asia prefer Ayurvedic medicines to deal with vagus nerve stimulation because they prove to be helpful in doing so. There are countless doctors that prescribe Ayurvedic medicines too. This is prevalent in India.

7. Connection or a Good relation: Forming healthy connections with friends and family members also help triggering the energy to flood the vagus nerve. This interaction causes the mind to slow down and relax which is a good thing when a person is too much involved in the modern world that gives nothing but

stress, anxiety and tension. The person feels good around people who love them or whom they love, according to a study research.

8. Fast intermittently: When you fast, it causes reduction in the number of calories that we intake since we don't eat as much as we do in our normal routines, well, come on, you know that fasting works like that. This is responsible for bringing variation in heart rate and also in the metabolism which causes the vagus nerve to function well. Hence, it is easily stimulated and causes the body and mind of the person to stay healthy and active.

9. Valsalva maneuver: This method requires you to breathe through the closed airway by pinching your nose close and joining your lips to keep your mouth shut. This way, the air would have no passage to pass through which would increase the pressure in your chest cavity which would ultimately increase the vagal tone.

10. Make use of a chewing gum: The chewing gum shoots the hormone CCK which helps strengthen the communication between the vagus nerve and the brain. Or in other words, when the person is constantly chewing gum, the mouth performs the same action over and over which results in the release of the hormone known as CCK, it keeps the vagus

nerve in action thus, it is stimulated on its own accord. Well, lucky for you if you have a habit of keeping chewing gum in your purse or your pocket.

11. Make use of more fiber in your meals: Eating fibers increase the hormone GLP-1 secretion which results in quick activation of the vagus nerve that gives the feeling of a full stomach for a long time. The foods that are rich in fiber include pasta, whole wheat bread, potatoes (with skin), nuts, carrot, peas, beans, berries, pulses, seeds, oats, sweet corn, etc. You can have a diet plan made and enjoy a healthy life!

12. Loud gargling with water: Gargling with water, mainly the cold water keeps the vagus nerve activated. This quickly stimulates the vagus nerve which causes the brain to give orders to the organs that seem to be malfunctioning to calm down and work well as needed. Engaging the larynx is the key here which quickly energizes the vagus nerve and keeps the person's inside healthy.

13. Get direct sunlight: The UVA rays that hit you when you step out in the sunlight cause you great benefits whilst you just walk squinting your eyes. You didn't know that, did you? Well, the sun rays activate the MSH hormone which abruptly stimulates the vagus nerve. Remember that your body likes it because the sun rays stimulate your vagus nerve.

14. Contract the stomach muscles or cough: You don't believe it, do you? Well, that's true. The coughing causes the muscles of the stomach to contract which causes the vagus nerve to be electrified. Well, cough all you want to stimulate your vagus nerve, but make sure, you don't get carried away.

15. Increase the consumption of seafood: Are you obsessed with prawns and sushi? Well, there's good news for you! There are benefits that lie in the seafood you devour! The vagus nerve is stimulated through the EPA and DHA found in the seafood. And you know what it does? Well, these two chemicals are responsible to improve the heart rate through the stimulated vagus nerve.

16. Letting saliva do its job: You must be wondering what a weird method it is but trust me, it works! All you have to do is let your saliva fill your mouth and then dart your tongue around to produce a hyper-relaxing vagal response. Don't believe it? Well, you always have saliva in your mouth, gather it all now and try this method for yourself!

17. Have 'Nervana' around you most of the time: It is the technology that is specifically designed for the stimulation of the vagus nerve through electrical waves with music.

18. For diabetic patients, insulin works as a catalyst to halt the glucose release from the liver and ultimately stimulating the vagus nerve.

19. Exercise regularly: When people are habitual of exercise, they benefit their vagal index and have a healthy life.

20. Have massages very often: Mostly the neck and the foot massages are responsible to trigger the vagus nerve stimulation and that results in seizures risk reduction and prevention from heart diseases. One could use the OSEA's aromatic Vagus Nerve Oil to massage your neck while focusing along the carotid sinus.

21. Sleep on the right side: It is a very easy and effective natural method to stimulate the vagus nerve.

22. Take zinc and serotonin supplement (5 H-T-P): The intake of zinc and serotonin is crucial in kick-starting the vagus nerve stimulation.

These are the vagus nerve stimulating methods that are natural and any individual can do it and have their vagus nerve activated successfully but when they fail to energize it, there is a surgical method for it which easily activates the vagus nerve without much hassle. That process is called VNS (Vagus Nerve Stimulation) Implant and it is done through a minor surgery using a unique VNS device approved by FDA.

Chapter 4 Healing Benefits

It Helps Prevent Inflammation

Just what is inflammation? Isn't it supposed to be useful? Why exactly is it thought of as something that is harmful?

To understand the questions above, we need to know more about inflammation, so our first question should be...

What Is Inflammation?

Inflammation is just one step in the process of healing. When your body is attacked by external forces, such as toxins, injuries, and infections that enter the body through openings or damages to the skin, then inflammation is a way for the body to fight against those forces. The body activates it when something damages or attacks your cells. It begins the process of inflammation by first releasing chemicals that encourage the immune system to respond. When the immune system responds, it releases proteins and antibodies while also decreasing the flow of blood to the affected area.

The entire process of inflammation usually lasts anywhere from a few hours to a few days. In such cases, we usually refer to the process as acute inflammation.

So far, so good. Your body is only using its natural defense mechanisms to heal you. However, things take a turn for the worst when the immune response lingers for a long time. When it does, the body is forced to stay in a constant state of alertness. This adds extra stress on the body. Think of this situation like stretching a rubber band to its limit but not letting it fall back to its original state of rest. The body is the rubber band, but the difference here is that while the rubber band does not feel anything, the body is not meant to be so stressed for long periods of time.

The state of stress is called chronic inflammation and it creates all kinds of trouble to the body, down to the organs and the tissues.

Acute Versus Chronic Inflammation: The Signs

When your body is going through the acute inflammation process, then you will notice symptoms such as swelling, redness, and pain in the area of damage. These symptoms are nothing you should be panicked about; they are part of the natural process of healing.

On the other hand, chronic inflammation has some serious symptoms. Here are some:

- Chest pain

- Fatigue

- Mouth sores

- Abdominal pain

- Fever

- Rashes

And yes, those are just some of them.

And no, that is not the worst part about chronic inflammation. The worst part is that the aforementioned symptoms can last for several months or years. Imagine going through abdominal pain for years.

The Cause Of Chronic Inflammation

There are several causes of chronic inflammation. The most obvious ones are listed below:

1. An acute inflammation response takes place and it goes untreated. For example, when you do not deal with an injury or infection, leaving it there to fester or worsen.

2. Acute inflammation could be caused by an autoimmune response. This is a response that occurs when your body turns in on itself. In such cases, the immune system mistakes healthy tissues and cells as invaders and decides to attack them. This happens when the body is trying to deal with the invaders and your tissues get caught in the attack.

3. You could also encourage chronic inflammation when your skin or a wound is exposed to irritants, such as pollution or industrial chemicals, for a long time. Eventually, your body does not get to rest because it is busy dealing with external forces constantly.

Now those are the obvious causes because you can see them develop on your body. Take the situation where your body is attacked by chemical substances. You can see the effects of it on the wound or injury. But not all causes are obvious. You might encourage chronic inflammation due to the below:

- Chronic stress

- Obesity

- Smoking

- Alcohol

In other words, you might not even be aware of the fact that you are causing chronic inflammation.

When Things Get Worse: How Chronic Inflammation Affects Our Body

Think again about or look back at the list of symptoms of chronic inflammation. Those symptoms only touch the tip of the symptom iceberg. The real problems occur as the inflammation worsens because when it does, it targets healthy organs, tissues, and cells. It does not stop there. Over time, as your organs, tissues, and cells continue to suffer, they lead to damage to your DNA, scarring within your body, and death of tissues. What you are left with are conditions that change your life completely. Conditions such as the below:

- Asthma

- Type 2 diabetes

- Cancer

- Heart disease

- Various neurodegenerative diseases, including Alzheimer's

How Is The Vagus Nerve Involved In All This?

The vagus nerve is one of the major control centers of the body and one of the most vital components of the parasympathetic nervous system. The health of the nerve eventually dictates the health of the immune system, the brain, and the overall inflammatory state.

But just how does it affect the inflammatory response?

For this, we have to turn to a special feature of the nervous system called the parasympathetic relaxation response.

Let's say that your body has now encountered a threat in the environment. Your brain perceives said threat and sends signals to various parts of the body, activating the fight-or-flight response. This puts the body into a state of stress, as it is now performing in overdrive mode. The benefit is that your reaction times and awareness have been enhanced. It almost feels like you have some sort of superpower. Despite the state of stress you are in after your body feels the effects of working too hard, it is necessary for you to deal with the situation. Now suppose that you realize that the threat in the environment is no cause for being alert. You might have assumed that a shadow you just saw was a prowler, but it eventually turned out to be an innocent teenager wearing headphones. No worries there. Time to calm down. (Unless in your world, innocent teenagers wearing headphones are something to be wary about.)

You are now ready to calm down. Biologically, your body is supposed to respond to the stress, realize that the threat has passed and then calm down immediately. The brain created the fight-or-flight instincts. But it is the vagus nerve that plays the primary role in activating the parasympathetic relaxation response. It is simply the vagus nerve's way of saying, "Stop! It is only a teenager with headphones. No need to be alarmed. The threat has passed." And to do this, the vagus nerve stimulates the release of acetylcholine, a neurotransmitter that is the body's equivalent of "hitting the brakes" on the inflammation response, which also gets activated when you enter fight-or-flight.

With that, your body begins to relax. Your breathing starts slowing down. Your heartbeat, which was thumping like a drum solo in a rock concert, starts to return back to a calm rhythm.

Here is a key point to remember. The vagus nerve releases acetylcholine for the main purpose of stopping the inflammation process, whether it is caused by your fight-or-flight response or not. In other words, when your body is healing and if it reaches a point when injury or damage does not pose a threat, then acetylcholine stops the inflammation process.

The strength of the vagus nerve's response—or in other words, how well it can stop the inflammatory process—is called the vagus tone. When the vagus tone is low, your inflammation becomes chronic because the system responsible for telling your body to calm down does not have enough power to do so. It went from being the boss of your body's organization to a mid-level employee.

With a high vagus tone, you make sure to manage the levels of inflammation in the body.

It Assists in Making Memories

Memories. They help us relive our fondest moments, assist us when we are solving problems, help us recognize people, or simply guide us back to our homes by showing us the right route to follow. Memories are an important component in our lives and the study of memories has yielded some interesting results.

Most people think that memories are only confined to a certain area or a few areas of the brain. It's like how we place wardrobes in our homes; you don't usually find one in the kitchen and one in the bathroom for good measure. They are stored in certain areas and they contain your clothing and valuables. However, memories are also related to the connections between neurons. In other words, a particular pattern in the neural network of your brain activates a certain memory.

This makes memories more complex than we originally thought. Let's take an example. When you recall something from the past, you are not simply plucking out random information and making use of it. Rather, you are recollecting the original pattern that was created when you first created the memory. This process of re-establishing a pattern is known as "pattern completion."

But why is this all important to know?

One reason: it takes more than just the brain to help us manage our memories.

The Vagus Nerve and the Memory, According to the APA

The American Psychological Association has provided some interesting results on the idea of memory and how it is linked to the vagus nerve (Adelson, 2004). Based on research conducted by psychologists at the University of Virginia, the vagus nerve, when stimulated, releases a certain neurotransmitter called norepinephrine into the amygdala, the primary part of the brain that assists us with emotions and memory. However, do bear in mind that the amygdala is not the only part of the brain that deals with memory.

This allows us to respond to certain events, situations, or experiences in emotional ways. In other words, we end up having a more emotional and meaningful response, which helps us strengthen our memory. It is common knowledge among the scientific community that emotions actually help us strengthen our memories (Tyng, Amin, Saad & Malik, 2017). This is best illustrated with an example. Let us suppose that you are taking a walk in the park. As you make your way down its twisted paths, you encounter a cat. There is nothing remarkable about the cat;

it is a stray cat just like the dozens that live in the park. Its only distinguishing feature is its color, but even that seems like something not worth paying attention to. A stray is a stray, doesn't matter what shade of fur it has. You promptly ignore it and go about your way, burying that incident in the countless memories that you have stored in the depths of your brain where they cannot be easily reached.

However, let's add a new element to the incident. This time, as you pass by the cat, you suddenly feel a surge of sadness coursing through you. When you near the cat, you feel like you just want to take it home. Alas! Your building's rules are strict about bringing pets into the apartment. You feel terrible about leaving the cat, but for now, there is nothing that you can do about the situation. Maybe you could carry some cat food with you, in case you encounter a stray in the park.

Remember how we understood earlier that memories are not just blocks of incidents stored in your brain, but patterns created between neurons? In the first scenario of the example above, you create a certain pattern for your memory. It is unremarkable and is easily forgotten. However, in the second scenario, you reacted to the situation in an emotional manner, thereby creating a more complex pattern. Because the pattern is complex, it also becomes unique.

In the future, it becomes easier for your brain to recollect the incident. In fact, the incident can influence your future actions.

You could be motivated to change your apartment so you can find a place where they accept pets.

All of this is possible because your vagus nerve influences the creation of neurotransmitters after an emotional response and through that your brain creates memories that can be recalled easily.

It Controls Your Heart Rate and Blood Pressure

We know that the vagus nerve is a wandering nerve. It may start from the brain, but it branches out to influence many organs and processes. One such organ is the heart.

It is wrong to say that the vagus nerve is directly connected to the heart. If that was the case, then we would suffer a cardiac arrest if the nerve sustained damage. Rather, the nerve is connected to the muscles that are connected to the heart. When the brain sends signals to the vagus nerve, it reacts to those signals and then transfers them over to the muscles near the heart. This, in turn, lets your heart know that it should slow down.

But how does it all work?

Let's think about it this way. You suddenly realize that you are late for an interview. As you step outside your building, the first thing that you set your eyes upon is the traffic that extends all the way to your destination. Thankfully, you know that you just have to walk three blocks to reach the place of your interview. So you decide to run. Your brain sends a signal to the muscles of your heart to pump more blood. This gives you a boost of energy and you sprint over to your place of destination. Once you reach there, you pause to catch your breath. You don't need your heart to beat fast anymore. Your brain understands this and sends a signal to the vagus nerve. It then communicates the message to the muscles surrounding the heart to slow down the heart rate.

This slowing down process also occurs when you are feeling nervous or anxious. Once you have calmed yourself down, your vagus nerve sends the right signals to inform your heart to return to its normal rate of beats.

But what about blood pressure? How does the vagus nerve treat your blood pressure?

To understand that, let us try and wrap our heads around blood pressure. In many cases, people can live their lives with high blood pressure and not even realize that something is wrong. This prevents people from seeking medical attention because they are under the impression that everything is normal.

There are many causes for an increase in blood pressure. Blood pressure simply indicates the amount of blood that is passing through the blood vessels. We also look at the resistance that the blood encounters as the heart continues to pump the blood into the body.

One of the causes for the increase in resistance is narrow arteries. When blood tries to pass through these arteries, then it does not flow freely. This causes the amount of blood that is transported to various parts of the body to decrease.

No one can notice the change occurring in their system. But they do notice the below symptoms.

- Headaches
- Shortness of breath
- Nosebleeds
- flushing
- Dizziness
- Visual changes
- Blood in the urine

One of the ways to check for blood pressure is to go and take regular readings. This way, you can detect it before it becomes something worse.

However, what if you want to keep your blood pressure at manageable levels? What if you want to avoid repeated visits to the doctor? What if you don't want to wait there in the examination room as the doctor goes over your charts and you are probably thinking of all the situations in the past six months that could potentially cause a spike in your blood pressure?

You take care of your vagus nerve.

When your brain notices your blood pressure level rising, then it immediately sends a signal to the vagus nerve. Since the nerve influences the heartbeat, which eventually influences the amount of blood being pumped at one time, it lowers the heartbeat slightly. This process allows for a decrease in blood pressure to prevent any further harm to the body.

Simple isn't it? However, there are two key things to note at this point.

- While the vagus nerve prevents the blood pressure from increasing, it really is a stop-gap solution. You need to still deal with the underlying problem that caused an increase in blood pressure.

- The vagus nerve also needs to be taken care of. This means that you have to focus on improving the condition of the vagus nerve.

The vagus nerve has a lot of influence on our body and does what it can to prevent problems from escalating. However, it cannot perform the tasks alone. You need to work alongside the nerve and make sure that you are taking care of it as it takes care of your body.

Chapter 5 The Role Of The Vagus Nerve In Depression

The etiopathogenesis of misery is a profoundly perplexing procedure portrayed by a few neurobiological adjustments incorporating diminished monoamine neurotransmission in the cerebrum, dysregulated hypothalamic-pituitary-adrenal hub action, diminished neuronal versatility, and incessant aggravation in the mind and fringe tissues. Trial and clinical examinations show that the vagus nerve may impact these procedures. The significance of the vagus nerve in the etiopathogenesis of wretchedness is additionally bolstered by its association in the enlistment of affliction conduct, just as by clinical examinations affirming a valuable impact of vagus nerve incitement in discouraged patients. The point of this article is to portray current information of afferent and efferent vagal pathways job in the improvement and movement of despondency.

For reasons that specialists don't totally comprehend, these electrical driving forces transmitted by means of the vagus nerve to the cerebrum can assuage the indications of discouragement. The driving forces may influence the way nerve cell circuits transmit flags in territories of the cerebrum that influence temperament. Nonetheless, it more often than not takes a while before you feel the impacts.

At whatever point it's fundamental, your primary care physician can change the settings on the gadget (basically changing the portion) in the workplace with a programming wand. Ordinarily, the gadget is set to go off at normal intervals. You can likewise turn it off utilizing an extraordinary magnet.

Vagus nerve incitement includes the utilization of a gadget to invigorate the vagus nerve with electrical driving forces. An implantable vagus nerve trigger is as of now FDA-affirmed to treat epilepsy and despondency.

In ordinary vagus nerve incitement, a gadget is carefully embedded under the skin on your chest, and a wire is strung under your skin interfacing the gadget to one side of the vagus nerve. At the point when initiated, the gadget sends an electrical flag along the left vagus nerve to your brainstem, which at that point sends a sign to specific regions in your mind. The correct vagus nerve isn't utilized in light of the fact that it's bound to convey strands that supply nerves to the heart.

New, noninvasive vagus nerve incitement gadgets, which don't require careful implantation, have been affirmed in Europe to treat epilepsy, wretchedness, and agony. A non-invasive gadget that animates the vagus nerve was as of late endorsed by the Food and Drug Administration for the treatment of bunch cerebral pains in the United States.

Vagus Nerve Incitement

Around 33% of individuals with epilepsy don't completely react to hostile seizure drugs. Vagus nerve incitement might be an alternative to decrease the recurrence of seizures in individuals who haven't accomplished control with prescriptions.

Vagus nerve incitement may likewise be useful for individuals who haven't reacted to concentrated despondency medicines, for example, upper meds, mental guiding (psychotherapy) and electroconvulsive treatment (ECT).

The Food and Drug Administration (FDA) has affirmed vagus nerve incitement for individuals who:

- Are 4 years of age and more established?

- Have central (halfway) epilepsy

- Have seizures that aren't well-controlled with prescriptions

The FDA has additionally affirmed vagus nerve incitement for the treatment of melancholy in grown-ups who:

- Have incessant, difficult to-treat despondency (treatment-safe melancholy)

- Haven't improved in the wake of at least four drugs or electroconvulsive treatment (ECT), or both

- Continue standard sorrow medications alongside vagus nerve incitement

Also, analysts are contemplating vagus nerve incitement as a potential treatment for an assortment of conditions, including migraines, rheumatoid joint inflammation, fiery inside ailment, bipolar issue, stoutness and Alzheimer's ailment.

Dangers

For the vast majority, vagus nerve incitement is protected. In any case, it has a few dangers, both from the medical procedure to embed the gadget and from the mind incitement.

Medical procedure dangers

Careful difficulties with embedded vagus nerve incitement are uncommon and are like the perils of having different kinds of medical procedure. They include:

- Pain where the cut (entry point) is made to embed the gadget

- Infection

- Difficulty gulping

- Vocal line loss of motion, which is generally transitory, however can be lasting

Reactions After Medical Procedure

A portion of the reactions and medical issues related with embedded vagus nerve incitement can include:

- Voice changes

- Hoarseness

- Throat torment

- Cough

- Headaches

- Shortness of breath

- Tingling or prickling of the skin

- Insomnia

- Worsening of rest apnea

For a great many people, reactions are mediocre. They may decrease after some time, yet some symptoms may stay annoying for whatever length of time that you utilize embedded vagus nerve incitement.

Changing the electrical driving forces can help limit these impacts. In the event that reactions are terrible, the gadget can be stopped briefly or for all time.

How You Get Ready

It's critical to painstakingly consider the advantages and disadvantages of embedded vagus nerve incitement before choosing to have the methodology. Ensure you recognize what the majority of your other treatment decisions are and that you and your primary care physician both feel that embedded vagus nerve incitement is the best alternative for you. Ask your primary care physician precisely what you ought to expect during medical procedure and after the beat generator is set up.

Nourishment and Prescriptions

You may need to quit taking certain prescriptions early, and your PCP may ask you not to eat the night prior to the methodology.

What You Can Anticipate Prior to the Methodology

Prior to medical procedure, your primary care physician will do a physical assessment. You may need blood tests or different tests to ensure you don't have any wellbeing worries that may be an issue. Your PCP may have you start taking anti-microbials before medical procedure to forestall contamination.

During The Strategy

Medical procedure to embed the vagus nerve incitement gadget should be possible on an outpatient premise; however, a few specialists suggest remaining medium-term.

The medical procedure, as a rule, takes an hour to 90 minutes. You may stay alert, however have drugs to numb the medical procedure zone (nearby anesthesia), or you might be oblivious during the medical procedure (general anesthesia).

The medical procedure itself doesn't include your cerebrum. Two entry points are made: one on your chest or in the armpit (axillary) locale, and the other on the left half of the neck.

The beat generator is embedded in the upper left half of your chest. The gadget is intended to be a perpetual embed, yet it tends to be expelled if vital.

After The Technique

The beat generator is turned on during a visit to your primary care physician's office half a month after medical procedure. At that point, it very well may be customized to convey electrical motivations to the vagus nerve at different terms, frequencies, and flows. Vagus nerve incitement typically begins at a low level and is step by step expanded, contingent upon your indications and symptoms.

Incitement is modified to turn on and off in explicit cycles —, for example, 30 seconds on, five minutes off. You may make them shiver sensations or slight genuine annoyance and transitory responses when the nerve incitement is on.

The trigger doesn't distinguish seizure action or melancholy side effects. At the point when it's turned on, the trigger turns on and off at the interims chosen by your primary care physician. You can utilize a hand-held magnet to start incitement at an alternate time, for instance, on the off chance that you sense an approaching seizure.

The magnet can likewise be utilized to incidentally mood-kill the vagus nerve incitement, which might be essential when you do certain exercises, for example, open talking, singing or working out, or when you're eating on the off chance that you have gulping issues.

You'll have to visit your primary care physician occasionally to ensure that the beat generator is working accurately and that it hasn't moved out of position. Check with your PCP before having any medicinal tests, for example, attractive reverberation imaging (MRI), which may meddle with your gadget.

Results

Embedded vagus nerve incitement isn't a solution for epilepsy. The vast majority with epilepsy won't quit having seizures or taking epilepsy drugs through and through after the method. Yet, many will have less seizures, up to 20 to 50 percent less. Seizure force may reduce too.

Vagus nerve incitement may likewise abbreviate the recuperation time after a seizure. Individuals who've had vagus nerve incitement to treat epilepsy may likewise encounter enhancements in state of mind and personal satisfaction.

Research is as yet blended on the advantages of embedded vagus nerve incitement for the treatment of misery. A few investigations recommend the advantages of vagus nerve incitement for wretchedness gather after some time, and it might take at any rate a while of treatment before you see any upgrades in your downturn side effects. Embedded vagus nerve incitement doesn't work for everyone, and it isn't proposed to supplant conventional medications. Moreover, some medical coverage bearers may not pay for this strategy.

Investigations of embedded vagus nerve incitement as a treatment for conditions, for example, Alzheimer's infection, cerebral pains, and rheumatoid joint inflammation have been too little to even think about drawing any authoritative decisions about how well it might function for those issues. More research is required.

Chapter 6 Other Functions

The vagus nerve, when used to its full potential, can have extremely positive effects in combating a host of physical and mental diseases, including migraines, depression, PTSD, inflammation, trauma, fibromyalgia, and a number of other diseases. Yes, mental illness is very much real and has physical components that come from it. It is not simply a thinking disease. We will break down the various diseases individually and discuss how the vagus nerve can be used to positively affect them.

We have really gotten in-depth on what the vagus nerve is, what it does, how it relates to the rest of the body, and how stimulating it can have immense health benefits and improve our overall well-being. We also described in detail what the effects of an unhealthy vagus nerve are. For this reason, we must do our best to keep the vagus nerve healthy. The vagus nerve is a critical juncture in the human body, and it cannot be ignored when trying to improve health and avoid disease. Continued research on the vagus nerve has shown that utilizing it to its full ability will be a great benefit to anyone who is willing to harness it. We hope that you know more about it now. Since we understand how many physiological processes the nerve moderates. We will now get into how many illnesses it can improve.

Vagus Nerve And Migraines

Migraines, for lack of a better phrase, really create a headache for us. They can really slow us down and impact our lifestyles. Many people suffer from migraines to the point they need to seek medical help and even get admitted to the hospital. Think about how a headache makes you feel. A bad enough headache will make you feel like you don't want to do anything at all. They negatively affect your activities of daily living, and having one every day would be like torture. Migraines are basically a recurring headache. They often occur on one side of the head, create a throbbing sensation, and may have a genetic predisposition. This is true for a small percentage of the population. Migraines can also be triggered by things like smells, lights, noises, certain foods, medication, lack of sleep, alcohol, tobacco use and a wealth of other sources. Whatever the cause of a migraine may be, they are absolutely no fun to have, and if we can help eliminate them in some way, it will absolutely benefit many people. No matter how big and tough you are, a bad migraine can put you out of commission easily. It is a pain even the toughest among us cannot handle for too long.

The vagus nerve can be used to help eliminate or reduce migraines significantly. The best part is, we all have a vagus nerve and can use it. The case is still out on whether vagus nerve stimulation can help with migraines. However, several research studies show that people who received vagus nerve stimulation over multiple years reported a significant improvement in their migraines. This was both in frequency and pain level. A survey that was conducted by Southern Illinois University for individuals who received vagus nerve stimulation for epilepsy, also showed that multiple people who had migraines prior to the therapy reported vast improvements in frequency and pain levels. Basically, all of the people who did have migraines prior to the therapies report vast improvements afterward. This is a strong indication that vagus nerve stimulation significantly impacts migraines in a positive way. Of course, these stimulations were done medically using implanted devices. However, many of the techniques we use can still have minor, indirect effects.

Many other prominent studies have shown that stimulation of the vagus nerve, including the noninvasive approach, significantly reduced migraines for a large number of individuals. This further cements that direct nerve stimulation is not necessary to help reduce migraines. The reporting in the reduction of pain is done by the patients themselves, which is really the strongest indication. If a person states they are not in pain, then they are not in pain. Many of these individuals also reported a higher quality of life due to the lack of pain. When a person has less pain, they are more likely to continue healthy practices as well.

A study done by a prominent neurologist in the early 2000s discusses a patient he had with chronic epileptic seizures. Unfortunately, for whatever reason, the Vagus nerve stimulation did not improve epilepsy. Not every therapy will work for every individual as each human organism is unique in its own way. This was an unfortunate circumstance for this patient. However, they were surprised to learn that the patient had a major reduction in his chronic migraines. Much to the joy of the patient. This was not the intended result, but since it worked, the treatment was partially successful. Researchers are continuing to do further studies on this phenomenon between the vagus nerve and migraines. It was really found by accident as multiple people who were getting treated for seizures using stimulation, surprisingly had an improvement in their migraines and headaches. The parasympathetic response of the vagus nerve seems to significantly reduce and even eliminate the causes of severe migraines. The parasympathetic response likely inhibits the overstimulation of the sympathetic nervous system in these cases, effectively altering the pain response. Vagus nerve stimulation also reduces stress, which can be a trigger for migraines. When the sympathetic nervous system is elevated, stress is increased. When the parasympathetic inhibitory response kicks in, stress, and in turn, pain, is significantly decreased

Go for a long walk or hit the gym. This may be difficult as exercise will be the last thing on your mind. As well, you can simply sit and take some deep breaths, hum or take a cold shower. Whatever you can do, try it out. Stimulating and utilizing the full potential of the vagus nerve can vastly improve migraines and improve your quality of life.

Vagus Nerve And PTSD

Post-Traumatic Stress Disorder, or PTSD, is a mental condition caused by a traumatic event that had a severe impact on someone. The people who are affected most commonly are in the military, law enforcement, first responders, or anyone in a field where tragedy is a common occurrence. However, PTSD may also strike just about anybody and everybody who has been through a traumatic event. A serious accident, death of a loved one, getting assaulted or any number of tragic events may cause a person to have PTSD. It may take years to overcome PTSD and some never overcome it at all. PTSD can manifest itself in multiple ways, including anxiety, anger, nervousness, negative thoughts, flashbacks, and chronic pain. They will often re-experience the trauma multiple times in their heads. There is a major split, even within the military community, whether or not PTSD is legitimate or not. For this reason, just like with depression, people will dismiss it as a non-issue. They believe that someone can just get over it. A person cannot just get over it though. PTSD is very real and is a serious mental disorder that needs to be treated as such. Unfortunately, PTSD continues to carry a negative stigma to it that can hopefully be a thing of the past once people start realizing some of the physical elements to it as well.

While there is no known cure for PTSD, there are therapies that may be used to help subside some of the signs and symptoms. Currently, some of the therapies include talk therapy and exposure therapy. Several studies suggest that vagus nerve stimulation may be a productive adjunct therapy for helping with PTSD, especially with the pain that is associated with it. A University of Texas, Dallas, and study researched the effects of vagus nerve stimulation on rats. The rats in this particular study were shown to display some signs that come with PTSD, like fear, aggression, and anxiety. A session of vagus nerve stimulation showed a significant reduction in these negative signs. Not only that, the signs did not return in many cases after another episode of trauma, suggesting that the stimulation may have more long-term effects than the other therapies. Researchers feel that if the stimulation can work in the same manner in humans, it may significantly reduce the pain associated with PTSD. If the effects are more long term as well, then it is certainly an adjunct therapy worth looking into.

If you have a friend or loved one who experiences PTSD, perhaps it is time to get to work on them. Help them by using the techniques that will stimulate their vagus nerve. That old cliché of "laughter is the best medicine" may be the ultimate tool in this situation. Help your loved one get regular exercise. Remember, this does not just mean going to the gym. Most people are more likely to do something if they enjoy it. Find something they want to do physically and help them do it. If they love playing basketball, play a quick pickup game. If they love going for walks, find a nice trail, and enjoy the sites. Whatever you can do to get them moving, do it. Finally, how about a nice round of karaoke? Singing and dancing are definitely a great way to stimulate the vagus nerve and get your friends out of the poor mental state they are in. If we can continue to correlate vagus nerve stimulation with helping to subside the signs of PTSD, then hopefully, we can remove the stigma associated with it as well. Just like with depression, we may never be able to cure PTSD, but we can certainly manage it with the appropriate practices.

We want to talk further about how PTSD can manifest itself into physical symptoms like muscle tightness, fatigue, and digestive issues. Many of these physical responses to a traumatic event indicate a sympathetic nervous system activity. Things like muscle tightness that is not heart-related often come from stress and being worked up for so long. They do not come from being in a relaxed state. Furthermore, fatigue develops when the body is overly stressed for long periods of time. This is why excessive sympathetic responses are not healthy for the body. If your body is in a constant state of pain and tiredness due to a traumatic event, then perhaps it is time to really start stimulating your vagus nerve to inactivate your parasympathetic response. The inhibition from the parasympathetic response will put your body in a state of relaxation, releasing the built-up tension and helping to reduce the pain associated with PTSD. Do this regularly, and it can really help to manage the negative signs and symptoms of Post-Traumatic Stress Disorder.

Chapter 7 What Is The Vagal Tone?

The Polyvagal Theory has effectively linked the physical and emotional. Physical actions can regulate emotional conditions; emotional activities can cause physical responses. For example, deep, forceful, diaphragmatic breathing can initiate a state of deep calm, while emotional reactions can lead to stress, triggering elevated heart rate and respiratory rates and a range of other visceral organ reactions, such as stopping digestion to conserve energy. Given the role of the vagus nerve in mediating both physical and emotional reactions, it is no surprise that the vagus nerve can be engaged to better manage our emotional sense of well-being and help alleviate physical problems.

As we have seen, under normal conditions, the calming parasympathetic nervous system is dominant, keeping the body in a state of homeostasis. In this context, vagal tone is an assessment of the body's readiness to perform certain key functions effectively. An ideal vagal tone maintains a baseline from inputs, via the vagus nerve, received from the parasympathetic nervous system. Among the most important vagal tone functions is controlling heart rate to keep it from beating too quickly. Vagal activity is key as well to controlling breathing rate, managing the rate of peristaltic contractions during digestion, and further affecting the sensitivities and inflammation of the digestive tract and functioning of the liver. Vagal tone is also a measurement of emotional stability, as emotions are at their baseline of normalcy when the dorsal vagal and ventral vagal responses are at homeostasis.

But this is not always the case, especially when emotional reaction ignites physiological responses.

Regulating Emotion

The parasympathetic nervous system follows two pathways. The better known, and far more dominant, is the ventral vagal pathway that controls most of the key organ functions. As noted above, it encourages social engagement and interaction to further secure and stabilize the individual. The more recently recognized but older pathway, the dorsal vagal, controls the emergency freeze response, which causes immobility, lightheadedness, speechlessness, fainting and shock. While the ventral vagal parasympathetic response is mediated by the neocortex, the newest and most developed part of the brain, the dorsal vagal parasympathetic response is mediated or activated by the most primitive, reptilian part of the brain.

Malfunctioning of either of these vagal pathways can lead to emotional disturbances, but regulating the vagal tone can moderate the disturbances. Brain function, specifically emotional responses and reactions, are directly affected by signals carried by the vagus nerve. Studies have shown that behavioral measures of emotional expression, emotional disturbances, self-regulatory skills, and reactivity may be correlated with baseline cardiovascular levels of vagal tone, leading to the conclusion that cardiovascular vagal tone can be an indicator of how well emotions are being regulated and managed. This perspective was not under consideration traditionally until the Polyvagal Theory opened this enlightened perspective and continues to encourage further experimentation.

The higher the level of vagal tone, the healthier the baseline condition of mind and body. Therefore, given the direct relationship between physical and emotional conditions, it follows that practicing the exercises to improve physical vagal tone will contribute to the improvement of emotional conditions, returning them to more normal baseline levels.

Emotional conditions that may be the consequence of low vagal tone include anxiety, depression, sensations of stress, fatigue not caused by excessive activity, and sleeplessness. Other, more long lasting emotional conditions may include Post Traumatic Stress Disorder (PTSD), and Attention Deficit Hyperactivity Disorder (ADHD). While many of these emotional disorders may respond to professional counseling and prescribed medication, hard-to-treat cases may respond favorably to vagal toning activities.

Physical actions that can return the body's emotional and physical reactions to normal baseline levels, include Yoga stretches and poses, various forms of meditation, oral exercises to stimulate the vagus nerve in proximity to the vocal cords, cold water to the face, auricular massaging of the ears and earlobes and sides of the neck to stimulate the vagus nerve as it passes through the ears and along the carotid arteries. Practicing mindfulness, or being in the moment, is a variation on meditation, with awareness of every environment stimulus.

The effectiveness of all of these exercises can be enhanced by managed, diaphragmatic breathing, with deep, deliberate, thoughtful inhales and exhales, which directly stimulate the vagus nerve. The effect is to slightly increase the heart rate on inhales, and then to lower heart rate back to a healthy, or homeostatic baseline on exhales.

When vagal tone is high, physical and emotional states are normal. Low vagal tone, the consequence of not stimulating the vagus nerve, can result in the range of emotional disorders we've been discussing and, additionally, can contribute to a sense of apathy, loneliness, isolation, and negative moods. These are all symptoms of the inability to engage socially and participate in social interaction. This may continue a self-perpetuating downward spiral, with the sense of isolation tending to discourage social interaction, and with the disconnection from social engagements furthering the feelings of isolation.

Low vagal tone can have equally serious consequences physically, including cardiovascular disorders.

Cardiovascular Applications

The relationship between the vagus nerve and the heart has been extensively researched and verified, with further clarification emerging from the Polyvagal Theory.

To set the stage for understanding this relationship, let's begin with the physical side of the relationship, keeping in mind that the vagus nerve is neither organ nor muscle, but is a long, multi-branched network of wire-like nerves connecting the brain and other organs, carrying the electrical impulse messages between them. This is how the vagus nerve carries messages that affect one of the most important physical elements, the heart, and does so every second, 24 hours every day.

The vagus nerve travels from the brainstem and connects with the heart muscle or myocardium on the upper right side of the heart, in a cluster of nerves called the sinus node, for short, or sinoatrial node. Here the vagus nerve acts like a natural pacemaker, regulating the heartbeat. During normal conditions, at times of homeostasis, when there is little or no activity or stress, signals arriving from the brain through the vagus nerve slow the heart rate to less than 100 beats per minute. It is subsequently slowed and regulated, sequentially, by the atrioventricular node, the bundle of His, the right and left bundle branches, and finally the Purkinje fibers at the bottom of the myocardium. Every second or so, the heart muscle contracts, blood is forced out of the ventricles toward the lungs from the right ventricle, and into the aorta from the left ventricle.

Now, here is where the relationship between the heart and emotional reactions occur, but first, a quick background. The Polyvagal Theory has added clarity to our understanding of how the autonomic nervous system in primates evolved from the more primitive reptile nervous system. Changes evolved to accommodate the more complex primate nervous system, resulting in increasingly elaborate vagal pathways that control or regulate the heart. There was a transition from the exclusive dorsal vagus nucleus among reptiles to a more elaborate structure in mammals, called the nuclear ambiguous.

This included a connection between the heart and the face that enabled social interactions to influence the visceral or bodily functions, and possible dysfunctions. In simple terms, this means that social activity and other emotionally-regulated activities could play a role in maintaining control over the heart rate, while conversely, cardiovascular events can directly affect the emotions.

Charles Darwin, the founder of evolutionary theory, recognized the bi-directional flow between the brain and the heart that is mediated by the vagus nerve. Darwin understood that facial expressions were a physical manifestation of emotions, and correctly surmised that there were neural pathways connecting the brain with the heart and other organs that would facilitate physiological responses to emotions. Darwin and those of his time were correct in their estimate, despite not yet knowing that the pneumogastric nerve, renamed the vagus nerve, had its own private network connection between the brain and the heart, apart from the connections of the action-oriented sympathetic nervous system. Capabilities to elevate and reduce heart rate coexist.

Today, Polyvagal Theory has led to discoveries of how vagal tone, the state of homeostasis, can be determined. A simple but effective determination of vagal tone is measurement of the heart rate during inhalation, when it should increase slightly above baseline, and then, measurement of the heart rate during exhalation, when the heart rate should return to baseline. The different rates of the two heart rates can be used to specify the precise vagal tone.

What Does This Mean To You?

During times of stress, your physical side may be in a state of elevated heart and respiratory rate, and you may be sweating, feeling a need to exert yourself and take action. In those situations, when the cause of the sympathetic response is alleviated, and there is no need to run, or fight, or jump, you can bring things down, calm your body, with thoughts of calm, peace, reassurance. Repeat to yourself that everything is cool, under control, and its okay to relax.

On a more serious medical level, when controlling heart rate and respiration are beyond the self-application of physical and emotional exercises, a relatively new treatment is the subcutaneous insertion of a vagus nerve stimulator. It is connected to the vagus nerve, and generates regular electrical impulses, acting like a pacemaker to increase vagal tone. Newer technologies have led to non-invasive electrical stimulators that make access to this treatment less expensive, and enables application to a wide range of symptoms. One of the first successful applications of electrical vagus nerve stimulation has been treatment of epilepsy, and up to 50% success in reduction in seizures has been achieved, among patients not responding to medication.

Autoimmune Responses And Inflammation

A relationship has been established between the autonomic nervous system (ANS) and the body's inflammatory response. It has long been understood that the autoimmune system includes inflammation among its responses to infection, since inflammation helps trigger many aspects of the body's defense, including release of macrophages or white blood cells, and killer T-cells that identify and annihilate invading microorganisms. But often the autoimmune system can overreact and overwork, continuing inflammation to the point that it can become damaging.

Non-drug treatments to calm the autoimmune responses are being derived from Polyvagal Theory. One approach is rocking, that is, a rocking motion in a chair or on a cushion. This is believed to have a soothing effect overall, and a stimulating effect on carotid baroreceptors. Recall that vagal tone can be increased by massaging the vagus nerve on both sides of the neck, where the vagus nerve runs past the carotid arteries. As a result of steady, continuous rocking several times a day for several days, blood pressure levels are lowered as the relaxation functions of the parasympathetic nervous system are engaged.

Another relaxant of the autoimmune response involves contractions of the pelvic floor, in a manner similar to contractions of the diaphragm. But while the diaphragm controls the upper body functions of the lungs and respiratory system, the pelvic floor affects the lower body, including the bladder and colon. An exercise to contract and engage the pelvic floor involves sitting on an exercise ball and feeling the pelvic floor begin to relax and settle into the ball, then trying to tighten it, then releasing it, letting it settle again, and repeating the cycle.

Dr. Stephan Porges, founder of Polyvagal Theory, also advocates standing on a half exercise ball with a rounded bottom and flat top, with someone else holding the person's hand to steady and give reassurance. This not only facilitates the therapeutic benefits of the balancing effort, it introduces a social engagement function, which signals the calming parasympathetic nervous system to initiate the socially engaging and relaxing ventral vagal response.

Added to these targeted, specific exercises can be the group of actions that have been used for other situations where the fight or flight sympathetic nervous system has engaged and needs to be turned down, or whenever the dorsal vagal response creates immobility, lightheadedness and more severe freeze symptoms. These include Yoga poses and stretches, meditation, vigorous cardiovascular exercises, massage of the neck and ears, cold facial therapy, and importantly, diaphragmatic deep, conscious breathing.

But in cases of more serious autoimmune disorders, there is no substitute for professional medical treatment. The critical first step is the correct diagnosis of the condition and identification of its cause.

Our contemporary ingestion of medications for numerous conditions, both real and imagined, can lead to bodily reactions, notably autoimmune overreactions. This may be exacerbated by taking herbal supplements, which can conflict with medications being taken, or that might initiate autoimmune disorders on their own:

Herbal supplements are lightly regulated by the Food and Drug Administration (FDA), and marketers may not be fully cognizant of potential side effects. Anyone taking prescription medications should check with their physician or pharmacist before mixing their medications with herbs.

Chapter 8 Polyvagal Theory

Polyvagal theory fully explains the way our autonomous nervous system (ANS) really works. In biological circles, these were named sympathetic and parasympathetic. While not totally invalid, there are a lot of holes in this view of what is a very complex system.

Polyvagal theory posits that there aren't two but three levels or states to the ANS. The most evolved state is the ventral state, followed by the sympathetic nervous system and then the dorsal state. This theory of our nervous system states that the vagus nerve is actually two completely different sets of circuits, with one overriding and influencing the other.

The two state theory considered the vagus nerve as being just one big nerve, and this is clearly incorrect. Such conclusions were brought about thanks to adhering to age old theories and from a failure to view the problem from different angles. Polyvagal theory changes all of that and helps us understand not only thenature of depression and anxiety better, but also their treatments.

The vagus nerve is at the center of polyvagal theory and we've looked at it in great detail this far. Let's now take a step back and consider the theory as a whole.

Thermostats

The best way to think of these three levels of the ANS is to liken them to a thermostat. The nerves in your body monitor your sensory responses and initiate the appropriate reaction. A good example of this is our physical reactions to our environment. When we feel cold, our body begins shivering. The muscle shivers produce additional heat. We can then place ourselves close to a source of heat or simply wear more layers of clothing to protect ourselves better.

The responses of our ANS can be hybrid as well. Hybrid here refers to a combination of two layers. Friendly competition is an example of a hybrid between the ventral circuit and the sympathetic nervous system. The result is a simulation of a fight or flight state but has none of the bad side effects

Together with the hybrid states, we have five states that the ANS operates in which a far more flexible model of behavioral response as is compared to the old relaxation versus stress model. Let's examine the ins and outs of the ANS a bit more and see how the cranial nerves play a role in all of this.

Neural Pathways

The first neural pathway, that is the ventral system, expresses itself through CN X (the vagus nerve) along with four other nerves, namely CN V, VII, IX and XI. This circuit promotes a soothing and relaxed feeling which makes us socially amiable and open. In addition to this, emotions such as joy, positivity, and love are associated with the ventral branch of the vagus nerve.

Behaviorally, it expresses itself through shared time and activities with friends, family, and loved ones. In evolutionary terms, cooperation increased our chances of survival and this is why social activity brings us a lot of positive emotions. Even introverts and loners (people who like being alone) need a basic level of social connection since this is hardwired into all of us, even if the degree to which we need this is different (Oschman, 2016). Talking, walking, singing, dancing together and so on are just expressions of this need as is making the decision to raise and nurture children.

The neural pathway is the sympathetic nervous system as you know. This can also be referred to as the spinal sympathetic chain since most of the information with regards to this state is passed to the relevant organs via spinal nerves. This is when we beat ourselves up for movement, whether it be towards fighting or fleeing. Either way, survival is the ultimate aim here.

You can also think of this state resulting from your body being mobilized by fear. Emotions such as fear, anger, rage, and so on are associated with this neural pathway. When the sympathetic nervous system proves unequal to the task of dealing with the challenge we face, the dorsal system kicks in and this is the third neural pathway.

When faced with imminent destruction, our brain decides to immobilize us and chooses to conserve whatever energy is left. As I highlighted earlier, immobilization can be an effective survival tactic in nature when the odds are highly against a creature. In human beings the emotions of helplessness, apathy, and hopelessness are associated with this pathway. Physically speaking, your blood pressure drops, your muscles become loose and bodily functions realign themselves as described earlier. You might even faint or go into shock.

The fight or flight response kicks the antelope into action once it realizes it is being hunted. As it realizes the pride is overcoming it and that death is near, an antelope usually goes limp.

A lion is not a scavenger and as it's about to bite into its prey it realizes that the prey is dead already and this short circuits the lion's killer instinct. It does not eat dead things thanks to an evolutionary association with disease and death and hence drops its prey and moves on. Moments after this happens, the antelope rises back up and goes back to doing whatever it is the antelopes do.

Similar suggestions have been made about avoiding tigers and bears, although the advice with regards to bears is iffy. Another good example of the dorsal circuit saving the day is when a porcupine rolls itself into a ball when a predator approaches, thus making it impossible for the predator to bite it (the porcupine) thanks to the quills sticking out.

There are two hybrid states as I mentioned earlier. The first hybrid state is when the ventral system combines with the sympathetic nervous system. This can be thought of as being a case of mobilization without fear. In this state the sympathetic system helps us mobilize our muscles and body in order to perform at our best while the ventral system ensures we remain on the right side of the rules and keep things within bounds.

It isn't just humans who play in this way. Puppies and dogs often play fight with one another and bark and growl at each other. However, there is no threat of harm implied in any of this. If you can be mobilized without fear, then you can be immobilized without it as well. This is when the dorsal state combines with the ventral state to produce a feeling of safety and intimacy. Lying down and cuddling with your partner is an example of this state.

The ultimate aim of the nervous system with all of these circuits is to maintain what is called homeostasis. Homeostasis refers to a state of dynamic equilibrium between a living organism and its environment. In other words, your reaction to your environment needs to be appropriate. Laughing at danger is a singularly un-homeostasis like behavior.

Neuroception

Neuroception was the term coined by Stephen Porges to describe the process by which neural circuits distinguish between safe and unsafe situations. The thing with neuroception is that it occurs outside of our conscious awareness (Oschman, 2016). In fact, it takes place in the deeply primitive portion of our brain and reacts automatically. Experiences of having a sixth sense and so on are examples of neuroception.

This doesn't mean our conscious mind doesn't pick up information. The decision making process is a complex interplay between the conscious and the subconscious portions of our brain. You can think of neuroception as being the processing of information that our conscious mind doesn't pick up. As such, it works a lot faster than conscious perception. How many times have you walked into a situation and just known something was wrong? Alternatively, how often have you started doing something and everything just felt right? This is neuroception in action.

As you can see, there is plenty of room for things to go wrong as well. If your neuroception is warped, then you'll end up categorizing a perfectly normal situation as being abnormal and everything you perceive will be colored by this initial thought. This is referred to as priming in psychological circles (Oschman, 2016). Priming can be thought of as defining the frame your mind is in. If you witness an act of kindness prior to walking into a tough negotiation, you're more likely to view the other side as being amicable to a win/win situation.

Chapter 9 High Vagal Tone Vs. Low Vagal Tone

Better blood sugar control, lower blood pressure leads to improved digestion through the production of digestive enzymes, the reduction of migraines, the decrease of stroke risk and heart disease are all improved by having a high vagal tone to improve the functions of the body systems.

Heart conditions, strokes, depression, diabetes, and inflammatory conditions are associated with low vagal tone.

The autoimmune diseases of lupus, multiple sclerosis, inflammatory bowel syndrome, and psoriasis are also associated with chronic inflammation.

Obesity

Feeling full and satisfied after a meal is an important role that the Vagus nerve plays. If we don't feel satiated and continually feel hungry, this could lead to obesity.

The Vagus nerve sends that signal to discontinue eating when we're full to the brain. It makes the brain aware that there is short-term energy to use. The integrity of the vagal system could be linked to obesity.

If the Vagus nerve is malfunctioning at its peak, the hunger signals may not work optimally causing weight gain and overeating.

Obesity has been linked with a number of diseases such as cardiovascular disease, high blood pressure, type 2 diabetes, joint disease, certain cancers, gallbladder, gallstones and more. Obesity itself is now considered a chronic disease because of its contribution to developing other diseases. Thus, it is critical that the Vagus nerve function properly and send the brain hunger signals.

Although there are those people who have never experienced a weight problem who judge people for being overweight and assume that they just have no self-control, there are times when a person eats from stress. The stress can be from a chaotic home situation, sexual assault (that can cause PTSD to develop), another traumatic situation (such as a mass shooting or military service overseas), or a job situation that cannot be remedied because jobs in their area are few and far between and they need to hold the job.

This is important to understand because it brings a whole new dimension of a person who is obese and is not "eating just to eat, "but eats from the stress and anxiety of what they have to deal with.

Memory Formation

Research studies have concluded that the release of norepinephrine into the amygdala and hippocampus – where the brain forms memory – occurs when the Vagus nerve is stimulated.

They work harder to accumulate memories due to the surge in norepinephrine occurring in our internal memory banks.

Additional studies – especially those that have been performed on a human subject – it can very well potentially form a link to Alzheimer's risk and treatment to vagal tone.

Gut-Brain Axis

Here is another connection in the body to the gut, the body's other control center. Gut bacteria, intestinal penetrability, and general gut health have a great impact on our brain and gut microorganism can stimulate the Vagus nerve, impacting behavior and the brain studies show.

Another connection to the gut is the feeling we get when we sense that things aren't quite right with a person or a situation, but we can't quite explain how we instinctively know. This is what we know as a gut feeling, the feeling that is a real one and not imagined.

Our gut has the ability to connect our feelings to our brain by sending a signal from our gut to the brain. This conveyance afforded by the Vagus nerve through the gut-brain alliance is crucial to our mental and emotional health.

Vagus Nerve And Other Organ Processes

The Vagus nerve interacts with many other organs in the body. They are:

Liver and pancreas – controls blood glucose balance and works to prevent diabetes

Bladder – helps the kidneys function properly, and increases blood flow, which improves percolation in the body

Spleen – target organs have inflammation reduced by the Vagus nerve activation

Gallbladder – aids in the release of bile. This helps the body break fat down as well as remove toxins

Fertility and orgasms in women are controlled by the Vagus nerve. If the nerve is blocked or inactive, it can cause disorder and imbalance to the mind and body.

Promotes Calm

Fight or flight mode occurs when cortisol, known as the stress hormone, is released in the body. Rest-and-digest mode comes about when the autonomic nervous system transmits the stress to the brain.

The release of prolactin, vasopressin, and oxytocin – all which calm us down - are released by the Vagus nerve sending signals to the brain. A strong vagal tone can elevate the tolerance of stress, which will result in recovery time from stress, emotional strain, injury, and illness.

Research has shown that a stimulated Vagus nerve has encouraging results for suppressing fear and anxiety (Alex, 2019).

Aging

The Vagus nerve corresponds with our aging and it observes our immune system and nervous system. This contributes directly to our longevity and health. Inflammatory conditions that can be introduced into our bodies as we age and are associated with stress, improper diet and not caring for ourselves as we should when we age.

This is one more way that we have the ability to keep healthy and active to prolong the aging process. Reducing stress and living a healthy lifestyle can help. We can help the Vagus nerve from aging prematurely with simple exercises that will be covered.

All of us age each day. We are unable to evade this fact of life. We can only take care of ourselves to the best of our ability.

Fight Or Flight Response

The Vagus nerve, an element of the parasympathetic nervous system, helps to resolve stress or threatening situations.

Our sympathetic system lets the body react to stimuli. This controls our fight and flight responses and prepares the body for action by providing quick access to reserved energy, advancing respiratory and heart functions, and giving us the ability to either fight or run from threats.

These stress reactions offset the effects of the parasympathetic system that gives us calm, rest and relaxation. These two systems work to develop a balance in the behavior of internal body organs and create a homeostatic state in the body.

The importance of the Vagus nerve cannot be stressed enough. It is the nerve that is vital to every organ that it interfaces with. It helps in the healing of depression and anxiety and certain illnesses, reducing the rate of our heartbeat and our blood pressure.

The Vagus nerve affects many of the sensory and motor functions in the body. A well-functioning Vagus nerve will keep the body in balance, while a malfunctioning Vagus nerve will need to be stimulated in order to bring balance back.

Chapter 10 The Relationship Of The Vagus Nerve With Other Nerves And Conventional Medicine

Just as the Vagus nerve interfaces with many of the organs in our body, it also interacts with other nerves in the nervous system. We know that the Vagus nerve sends signals to the brain from our organs and our senses and is the nerve of calm, helping to slow down our heart rate, reduce our blood pressure as well as stress levels.

Pain is another sensation that the Vagus nerve interfaces with and the nerve that is linked to pain is the trigeminal nerve, which carries sensory input from the face and teeth.

As you know, there are many, many people who have a fear of the dentist, even though the dentist can improve a person's health significantly. When we understand the basics of our nervous system and how anxiety, fear, and pain work and have an effect on the body, it can help decrease inflammation, minimize pain, and minimize our fear responses.

The comprehension of the communication of the Vagus nerve and the trigeminal nerve and the functions they perform, the fight or flight of the trigeminal and the relief of pain and relaxation of the Vagus can help in reducing the inflammation, pain, and fear.

The trigeminal contains connections to the Vagus nerve via the key sensory core where the Vagus nerve may be manipulated by the chewing reflexes

Role Of The Trigeminal Nerve

The trigeminal nerve is the largest cranial nerve. As we've learned, it carries sensory from the face and teeth as well as oral and nasal cavities, the greater portion of the scalp and is the motor to other facial muscles.

The nerves have proprioceptive nerve fibers from the extraocular and masticatory muscles and are part of the sympathetic nervous system.

The Vagus nerve's connection to this nerve allows the possibility to add to either feeling of fear, anxiety, anger, pain (the increase of inflammation) or the sense of peace and well-being.

The complicated communication between these two nerves has become clearer through current studies that have recorded their link because of stimulating nerve studies that are associated with neuropsychiatric disorder treatments.

Role Of The Vagus Nerve

As we know, the Vagus nerve has various tasks in the body – heart rate, blood pressure, gastrointestinal tract function, perspiration, speech, and muscles in the mouth.

The gag reflex is reduced while the nerve is working correctly. The heart rate slows, the gut is calm, and the breathing is normal. As we now know, the Vagus nerve tends to act below par causing a person to become dizzy or faint when they are under extreme stress.

The reduction of inflammation and regulating heart functions is the role the Vagus nerve plays. It also lowers the heart rate as mentioned before.

The research of Otto Loewi, the neuroscientist who first discovered the Vagus nerve, demonstrated that the nerves in the body emit neurotransmitters that affect receptors in target tissues.

Tests performed on frogs where Loewi exhibited that there is a secretion of neurotransmitters that are calming when the Vagus nerve is stimulated.

Emotional And Physical Effects

When the Vagus nerve is excessively activated, stress and anxiousness can create vasovagal syncope as a result of an abrupt drop in cardiac output. Women and young children are affected by vasovagal syncope more than other groups who experience a period of extreme stress or fear of the nervous system.

Mental Health Pain

Post-traumatic stress disorder (PTSD) occurs because of a traumatic situation or event. Intrusive memories, negative thoughts, chronic pain, and anxiety are experienced by those who suffer from this disorder. Usually, the condition is treated with psychotherapy in conjunction with anti-anxiety and anti-depressant medications.

A recent study exhibited the link between pain and mental health. It focused on how the experience of emotion may be influenced by the Vagus nerve. The test was to see whether the noninvasive stimulation of the Vagus nerve could be used as a technique to dampen the sensation of pain.

It has been considered that people and how their bodies, with certain differences – their sympathetic and autonomic systems - cope with pain and are likely to be vulnerable to post-traumatic stress disorder. The study performed was to find out if it would be possible to rewrite the 'mis-firing' as a way to control pain management.

Two groups of participants were established – half treated with two minutes of non-invasive nerve stimulations approximately ten minutes prior to heat stimulus, and the other half had mock stimulation.

The results of the study drew three key findings:

The stimulation of the Vagus nerve is reduced to stimulation by using heat in brain areas known to be significant for discriminative and sensory processes of pain, as well as in emotional pain centers.

Sweat measurements showed stimulation of the nerve changed the involuntary response to a heat stimulus that was painful. People who participated in the study by having their Vagus stimulated, showed their response to perspiring diminished in comparison with mock-treated participants.

The stimulation of the nerve stifles the centers of the brainstem that are usually significant for the responses of fight or flee are identified to regulate the perspiration response to pain.

It was discovered that some people, although already having their Vagus nerve stimulated, may need more stimulation to get the same outcomes. The frequencies that are necessary may change over time and the approach needs to be personalized and not based on a set level and frequencies of stimulation.

The stimulation of the Vagus nerve is an approach to pain management and a form of neuromodulation that also includes the stimulation of the spinal cord.

FDA approved a noninvasive stimulator to treat chronic and sporadic headaches and a migraine that was severe. A device that can be implanted has been approved in the treatment of epilepsy, as well as a stimulator tested in a trial to introduce the treatment of rheumatoid arthritis.

The side effects of implanted nerve stimulators include nausea, hoarseness, and shortness of breath. (Diego, 2019)

Nerve Stimulation To Replace Pill-Based Medicine

In conventional medicine visits are made to see the doctor, we're being tested for a number of issues that can be a problem – depression, epilepsy, rheumatoid arthritis, asthma – and are prescribed medications in tablet or capsule form to treat the problem.

Yet, while addressing the problem that you may have, you may be developing other problems due to the side effects some medications have on your body. Scientists and researchers have found what could be a replacement to the medicinal tablets or work in conjunction with them.

A small device about as large as a pacemaker is inserted just below the collarbone on the left side and designed to stimulate the Vagus nerve. The device is already treating some types of depression and epilepsy which have not done well in responding to traditional treatments with Vagus nerve stimulation (VNS). It is the hope that conditions treated using VNS can be expanded and open another method of treating conditions that are difficult to treat with conventional medicine.

Chapter 11 Vagus Nerve And Emotional Detachment

This amazing technique deals swiftly with all sorts of emotional pain and has an infinite number of applications. EFT has been around for quite a while and is now used in many hospitals and psych units throughout the world by professional psychologists and psychiatrists who are continuing to get very positive results with severe emotional pain and trauma.

There is no doubt that strong emotions can be very painful things and it is now recognized that emotion follows thought. This is why psychiatrists spend years talking about trauma and trying to uncover triggers and thoughts that cause bad feelings, depression, phobias and the like.

EFT is a great way to deal with all fear though you will have to be thorough. Really take a look at all the different aspects of that fear and treat each one with a very specific opening statement.

Emotional Freedom Technique (EFT) or tapping requires that you tap specific acupressure points on the torso, hands and on the head in order to clear energy blocks caused by negative emotions and feelings.

What you do is tap lightly on each of them. You get used to doing this very quickly, and when you have been using EFT for a while you can just do a few taps here and there, maybe on your collarbone or under your eye, for rapid relief.

Generally tapping involves two stages. In the first stage you are tapping to express the negative emotions. This stage of tapping will last as long as you have an emotional charge, continual tapping will bring that charge down to a minimal level.

The second stage includes reframing the condition positively where you choose a positive emotion or thought to replace the negative ones. The cool thing is you can't tap incorrectly; your intention is enough to make it work correctly. Even without tapping the right acupressure points, you will still release the negative energy from your body. Choose a negative emotion or feeling you wish to clear based on a situation that is troubling you. For example, you might be angry at your neighbor Tom for letting his dog poop in your backyard.

First, feel where in your body the negative emotions are contained and tap there. This may be one location or many. For example, as you tap, you might say, "I choose to be open", "I choose forgiveness", "I choose to let go and move on".

Alzheimer's

Neurodegenerative illnesses are triggered by the protracted activation of the microglia. This chronic activation creates a predisposition to degenerative diseases such as Alzheimer's and dementia. Alzheimer's is a cognitive disorder that is typically characterized by memory loss of memory, impairment of the cognitive ability, which ultimately leads to the progressive and gradual loss of behavioral and social engagement skills.

Alzheimer's causes systemic degeneration and death of brain cells. The net effect of this is the impairment of brain functions and cognitive abilities. Alzheimer's ultimately leads to dementia, which is a condition brought about by the decline in mental function that impairs the sufferer's ability to live and function normally. Alzheimer's presents as a progressive ailment starting with forgetfulness and memory loss and gradually resulting in the inability to perform even simple and straightforward tasks.

Our ability to perform simple physical tasks such as eating or bathing and cognitive functions such as memory, recognition of people and places, or operating machinery and tools is normally wired into our brains. This is why patients developing Alzheimer's will forget even their children's names or where they live and will be unable to do tasks that they were able to do before, such as driving. Deterioration of the brain cells inevitably causes us to lose our mental aptitude and erases most of what we know.

Alzheimer's is a distressing condition not only for a patient who slowly loses all notion of who they are but also for the family members who watch the gradual deterioration happen and the transformation of a person from an independent functional human being to a helpless person dependent on others. While there is no treatment that can cure Alzheimer's, there are therapies that are used to slow down the degeneration of brain cells.

Vagus nerve stimulation therapy can effectively inhibit the chronic microglia stimulation and thereby aid in slowing down neurodegeneration. Observations on the effect of vagus nerve stimulation on the microglia illustrate a morphological change that deters neurodegeneration in the brain cells. Microglia in patients with chronic inflammation shows fewer and shorter branches when compared to the microglia in a person with a healthy central nervous system where the parasympathetic responses of the vagal nervous system are able to mitigate overstimulation of the microglia.

Epilepsy

Epilepsy is a neurological disorder that is characterized by seizures that are triggered by abnormal brain activity. The abnormal brain activity interrupts the normal function of various organs which results in epileptic patients exhibiting the following symptoms;

• Uncontrollable jerking movements in the limbs

• Staring

• Confusion

• Loss of consciousness

Focal epileptic seizures are caused by abnormal activity in one part of the brain. These types of seizures may result in complete loss of consciousness where the patient becomes unresponsive to their environment, or they may not cause a lack of consciousness but cause involuntary jerking of limbs, dizziness, or alter smells and appearance of objects.

Generalized seizures result from abnormal brain activity in all parts of the brain. They can be in the form of;

• Petit mal seizures which normally affect children and tend to cause subtle body movements and may cause loss of consciousness

• Tonic seizures which affect muscles in the back, arms, and legs

• Atonic seizures typically cause loss of muscle control.

• Colonic seizures which affect the facial tissues, neck as well as the arms and manifest with jerking muscle movements during the seizure.

• Grand mal seizures can cause an abrupt loss of consciousness, jerking movements of the body, and in some cases, tongue biting.

The abnormal brain activity that brings about epileptic seizures may be due to other conditions such as stroke or head trauma. Infectious diseases that target the brain, such as meningitis and prenatal injury, can also result in seizures. Children with epilepsy may outgrow the condition as they grow older, while in some epileptic patients, lifelong treatment is necessary to control seizures.

Vagus nerve stimulation is a therapy used in the treatment of epilepsy that involves the use of a pulse generator to stimulate the nerve into calming and reducing abnormal brain activity, which causes seizures. The role of vagus nerve therapy in epilepsy is in reducing the intensity, frequency, and duration of seizures.

The calming effect of the vagus nerve serves to diminish and limit abnormal brain activity such that even when the epileptic seizures occur, they are mild and more manageable. While the vagus nerve stimulation therapy cannot cure epilepsy, it plays a significant role in managing seizures when used long term in conjunction with epileptic drugs.

You walk into a cafe. You are there to meet someone and your first reaction is to look around the cafe to find the person. As you walk towards this person, your face breaks into a smile.

Your brain understands the fact that you are about to meet someone you know. It recognizes the idea that you want to be in the presence of this person and creates positive messages. That itself is translated on your face and you react accordingly. So your ability to interact well socially also depends on your vagus nerve because when your brain sends the message for you to be happy, you need to react accordingly. Imagine if your brain is happy about a situation but you have a scowl on your face. That does not convey how you feel about the situation. This is where the vagus nerve comes into play. It takes the message from the brain and arranges your facial muscles to create the intended results. We end up having so many facial reactions to choose from. Because of the unique ability to use different facial reactions, people are capable of reacting to one scenario in different ways.

Let us take an example right here. You have two people in front of you, one of whom loves coffee while the other is not a fan of caffeine. There is a table in front of them and on that table lie two cups of coffee. Person A lifts up one cup, sniffs the drink, and makes a grimace. Person B eagerly takes a sip of the coffee and shows an expression of contentment.

As you can see, each person exhibited different unique reactions to coffee. That is possible because the vagus nerve can create a multitude of expressions to allow us to react accordingly when presented with something.

Because emotions actually affect our social interactions, the vagus nerve plays an important role in our social skills. After all, you do not want to look happy when someone informs you that she has been to the hospital recently.

The vagus nerve is also responsible for innervating the larynx. This helps those muscles that relax, tense, close, or open the vocal folds. In other words, the vagus nerve helps with your voice. It allows us to increase or decrease our pitch, which is important when it comes to emotions.

For example, when we are sad, we often speak in low voices. When we get angry (and I mean anger bordering on rage), then we tend to shout. The way our voice modulates says a lot about our emotions. You can notice this when you are talking to your friends or family. When you know a person well, you tend to know what a person is feeling just by the way they speak. When our brain reacts in a particular way, it reflects not just in visual cues which are expressed through facial expressions, but also in auditory cues in our speech patterns.

Chapter 12 Empathy, Socialization And Vagus Nerve

What is interesting about the vagus nerve is that it is stimulated by socialization.

Many of its functions are related to the adjustment of facial expression and voice tone, so your feelings are reflected in the way you speak and facial expressions and you can send messages to others.

It is also involved in the production of the adhesion hormone oxytocin. Oxytocin is an adhesion hormone that is secreted from lactation to sexual intercourse.

Therefore, it has been scientifically proven that active socialization and connections with other people can help reduce stress levels and prevent degenerative neurological diseases.

At the same time, when we face other people, the vagus nerve is activated and facial expressions need to be adjusted.

One way to stimulate the vagus nerve is to use specific facial movements in addition to healthy socialization.

At the same time, you may feel excessive empathy related to other people's problems. This is all the same and vagal stimulation can help you.

Often we cut to protect ourselves and avoid socialization so as not to be at risk, but learning to give a vague nerve a positive tone, in a healthy and positive way you can even feel connected with other people.

Some scientists associate the vagus nerve with emotions such as gratitude and compassion for themselves and others.

Conventional Medicine And Vagus Nerve

In the medical literature, the vagus nerve is treated extensively, but it is done superficially by simply analyzing what human anatomy suggests without understanding the actual meaning. This or other features

In fact: rarely related disorders of the vagus nerve are really thoroughly observed to find a correlation between them.

When talking about dysfunction that can be caused by the vagus nerve, this does not actually blame them, even if it caused them!

Illustrative example: The medical literature teaches that the vagus nerve can cause heartburn, but doctors prefer to take antacids rather than focus on vagal problems.

Likely examples include.

Is this supposed "cautious" cause probably due to the fact that the drug is not prescribed to treat the vagus nerve?

The ATLANTO method can reduce or permanently eliminate vagal compression. Those who have been treated have reported profound and significant positive effects on various systems of their bodies.

Once the problem is resolved, you can understand the true size of the problem and the various obstacles that compression can cause.

Digestive System And Vagus Nerve

The intestine groups together a set of segments that, in order to coexist with other elements of the digestive system, require special support by the act of the nervous system.

The nervous tissue does not only exist within the brain and the rest of the tissues of the central nervous system. The gastrointestinal tract, given its large size and functional complexity, depends on the extensive influence of nerve tissue to allow communication between its different components.

This can be achieved thanks to the presence of specialized cells attached to the wall of the intestine that as a whole is called the enteric nervous system.

Gastrointestinal reflexes

The fact that the digestive tract is so wide and that each of its parts fulfills a certain function to facilitate the digestion and absorption of nutrients, makes the coordination between all these structures is essential to carry out these tasks.

This can be achieved through the nerve reflexes that characterize this system. Some stimuli (often mechanical or chemical) in a certain part of the digestive tract can trigger reactions that result in the stimulation of a nerve pathway capable of coming into contact with other segments of the digestive tract and inducing a response in another distant segment depending on the stimulus initial.

For example, the distension of the stomach or small intestine when there is food inside them triggers a nervous reflex capable of inducing the evacuation of feces that are stored in the final portion of the colon and rectum. In fact, this mechanism partly explains why some people feel the need to evacuate after having eaten.

This phenomenon studied for many years is possible thanks to the presence of nerve signal integration centers that act as "executors" of a given response.

For example, the same stimulus mentioned in the example generates a nerve impulse that is transmitted to anatomical structures called "ganglia", which really are a space in which thousands of nerves from different pathways converge.

In these nodes, usually located in front of the spine, an interaction is established between neurons from the stomach and those that send signals to the colon or rectum. This is known as reflex arch and allows communication between different segments of the digestive tract.

Bowel and nervous system: the enteric nervous system

Intestine and nervous system

The entire gastrointestinal tract has a series of unique nerve fibers that, taken together, are called the enteric nervous system. It is distributed from the esophagus to the anus and contains about 100 million neurons.

This is characterized by being totally independent of the central nervous system (which includes the brain and other tissues), although they may share some similarities.

One of them is that the functional unit remains the neuron, which works through the transmission of electrical impulses and substances called neurotransmitters, which allow the control of all tissues. These neurons are finely organized throughout this system.

The formation of two groups of nerve cells called plexuses is what allows the proper regulation of gastrointestinal functions. The first one is the myenteric or Auerbach plexus, and the second is the submucosal or Meissner's plexus. The main difference between them is their location in the wall of the digestive tract.

All these neurons send projections to the muscle cells and glands belonging to the wall of the intestine. Thanks to this, the enteric nervous system can regulate intestinal transit and nutrient digestion (which is produced by the release of substances from the intestinal glands).

The autonomic nervous system

This is responsible for regulating all visceral functions (such as maintaining blood pressure or heart rate) through various nerves that come into contact with vital organs.

Anatomically and functionally it can be divided into the sympathetic and parasympathetic system. The first one is responsible for mediating the fight or flight responses (such as increased blood pressure, vasoconstriction and pupillary dilation) and the parasympathetic is responsible for counteracting all these effects, to bring the organism to a normal state

These systems also influence the gastrointestinal tract and the enteric nervous system. The release of certain neurotransmitters on these tissues allows to mediate a series of important responses, in which the parasympathetic system favors intestinal transit and the secretion of substances (such as gastric acid) while the sympathetic is responsible for antagonizing all these effects.

Although the nerves that participate in both systems do not originate directly in the brain, they do in structures that are quite related to this organ.

The sympathetic is formed by nerves that are born from some segments of the spinal cord at the height of the thorax and lumbar spine, while the parasympathetic is from a region immediately below the brain called the brainstem, which is a segment that connects the brain with the spinal cord.

It is important to consider that the main nerve corresponding to the parasympathetic system is called the vagus or pneumogastric nerve, which contributes most of the parasympathetic innervation to the intestine.

Brain Control And Vagus Nerve Stimulation System

The sensory fibers of the vagus nerve send signals from the heart, blood vessels, lungs, trachea, and gastrointestinal organs to the isolated nucleus of the brainstem (NTS) and send neurites through the isolated nuclei to multiple important points that can be activated in the brain.

The region regulates emotional, endocrine, cardiovascular, digestive and respiratory autonomic functions.

In 1988, American doctor Jacob Zavala believed that vagal stimulation could alter brain potential, thereby preventing or preventing epilepsy. In 1994, the European Union approved the use of vagus nerve stimulation to treat epilepsy. In 1997, the US FDA approved the NCP system developed by Cyberonics (invasive vagus nerve stimulation is used to treat epilepsy; in 2005, the FDA approved treatment for depression, 2015 Approved for the treatment of obesity in 1980.

The search for the vagus nerve is endless, and the vagus nerve research is growing in Japan and abroad. International studies have reported that stimulation of the vagus nerve by surgery can significantly improve symptoms such as depression, sleep disorders, gastrointestinal dysfunction, and cardiac dysfunction.

However, the method by which surgical invasion stimulates the vagus nerve has many drawbacks. For example, high surgical risks (side effects, sequelae, etc.), high prices (approximately 150,000-200,000 RMB), limited population (extreme patients only). Scientists have long been looking for alternative solutions.

After scientific demonstration and clinical research, non-invasive vagus nerve stimulation has become the latest hot spot in recent years. This program is preferred by international researchers and medical manufacturers to avoid the disadvantages of invasive vagus nerve stimulation.

Based on the uncommon feel of non-invasive vagus nerve stimulation, some people try to stimulate the vagus nerve through yoga, massage, meditation, music and more. With a specific music package to optimize, the vagus nerve achieves a soothing effect.

However, shallow stimulating effects are not obvious, and deep stimuli are expensive and risky. How to optimize the vagus nerve in a way that compromises between shallow and deep stimulation

Immune System And Vagus Nerve

As you age, the immune system causes more inflammation and the nervous system causes stress. That is how the immune system reacts to the heart. Our immune system is controlled by the vagus nerve.

The vagus nerve controls bone marrow cells that become liver, intestine, lung, or skin cells.

Our body has the ability to self-regulate, repair, regenerate and prosper as long as we learn to work with the body, not against the body.

Combining your mind and emotions with active practices such as meditation and equivalent can help with health and longevity. If you feel acute anxiety or stress, learning vagus nerve stimulation techniques can be very helpful.

What Link Between Inflammation And Allergies?

25 to 30% of the population is allergic to something. An allergy is a type of inflammatory reaction caused by the intrusion of an

allergen, that is, a compound that the body mistakenly equates to a threat.

The allergic reaction results from a hypersensitivity first established by a first exposure to the allergen (sensitization phase), then inflammatory reactions at each new exposure, unlike auto-inflammatory and autoimmune diseases, allergies are caused by a compound outside the body, not a constitutive dysfunction. Allergies are treated with seasonal antihistamines or desensitization in the allergist.

An infection refers to the intrusion of a pathogen (virus, bacteria, parasite ...) into the body. The infection can be caused by ingestion, inhalation, contamination of an injury, sexual intercourse, etc. and can cause an inflammatory reaction

We know that inflammatory responses play a fundamental role in the development and persistence of many diseases and can lead to debilitating chronic pain.

In most cases, inflammation is the body's natural response to a type of stress. But if the chances of stress that cause the "fight or flight" reaction of the nervous system and, therefore, less biological footprint of stressful stimuli, reduce inflammation, are reduced.

Anti-inflammatories are routinely prescribed to fight inflammation, but the evidence that vagus nerve stimulation and improvement of the "vagal tone" work is also increasing. A healthy and adequate "vagal tone" can be achieved through certain holistic therapies such as meditation, yoga, acupuncture or chiropractic among others.

A healthy vagal tone and positive emotions feed each other.

A deep diaphragmatic inhalation followed by a long exhalation is a key to stimulate the vagus nerve and slow heart rate and blood pressure.

The index of a high tone of the vagus nerve is related to physical and psychosocial well-being. And vice versa, a low index is related to inflammation and depression.

Chapter 13 Practical Self Help Exercises For Vagus Nerve Activation

Now that you know how the vagus nerve operates and why it is important for your health, let us now focus on its application. Many people are quick to use any means of vagus nerve activation that comes their way. As already mentioned, there are some techniques of vagus nerve activation that are helpful while others are harmful. You must be cautious not to use harmful techniques. Continuous activation of the vagus nerve using the wrong techniques may lead to chronic inflammation, which may be a source for more trouble. We have already looked at the negative effects associated with vagus nerve inflammation.

Breathing Techniques For Vagus Nerve Activation

To help activate the vagus nerve, you can adapt diaphragmatic breathing. In this type of breathing, the aim is to reduce the tension on the lungs and the heart. When you use this type of breathing, you allow yourself to take in air in slow bits that help reduce pressure. Diaphragmatic breathing helps in expanding the diaphragm. This is effective in reducing blood pressure and calming down nerves during anxious moments. The reduction of pressure and calming of nerves helps the body activate parasympathetic actions of the vagus nerve. The activation of parasympathetic action eventually leads to res

step guide to diaphragmatic breathing.

Step 1: Position Yourself

When you want to breathe and calm down your
align your body in a position that allows sufficient intake of air.
In simple terms, your lungs should be open. If you try
diaphragmatic breathing while you are lying on your belly or
sitting in a bad position, you will strain; your body should be free
enough to allow enough air into your lungs. The best positions
include when you are standing upright or when you are seated
upright. You can stand in an upright position and slightly spread
your arms. This posture opens up your chest to allow sufficient
air in. If you are seated on a chair or a mat, ensure that your back
is in an upright position. This allows you to freely inhale the air.

Step 2: Inhale and Pause

After positioning yourself strategically, inhale a large chunk of
air slowly and hold it in. You can hold your breath for about ten
seconds or even more. Given that regular breathing includes 10
- 14 inhalations per minute, the diaphragmatic breathing usually
involves around 6 inhalations per minute. When you inhale the
fresh air, do not be in a hurry to let it out. Hold on to it for a few
seconds; approximately 10, then release it gently.

: Slowly Exhale

After about ten seconds, you can now exhale and start the process all over. When you let out the air, you feel as if space has been freed up, and a weight has been lifted off your shoulders. The exhalation process helps clean your body of all negative energy. When you release the air, you allow your body to calm down and resume normal activities. It is important to note that this type of breathing should be well coordinated to work. If you do not allow yourself to calm down and try focusing on your breath, the effort may be worthless. As much as you want to enjoy your life and get rid of anxiety, you must try training your thoughts to focus on your breathing. You need to allow yourself to visualize the entire process.

Exercises That Activate Your Vagus Nerve

Exercising on a daily basis can also affect your vagus nerve. We know that physical activities are directly influential on your heart rate and blood pressure. These activities may moderate the heart rate or may increase it depending on your condition. While physical activities are effective in controlling the vagus nerve, not all activities will work out. In most cases, it is the gentle physical activities that do not require a lot of energy that works well in activating the vagus nerve. The two main physical activities used in vagus nerve activation include yoga and tai-chi.

Yoga: Yoga is a form of physical activity that involves stretching of the body muscles in combination with meditation and affirmation recitations. Yoga combines so many physiotherapeutic techniques in one session. If you want to benefit from the vagus nerve activation ability of yoga, you need to find the right yoga trainer. You can also perform yoga at home by using guided videos. One important factor to keep in mind when it comes to performing yoga is that the session should be mined calming. When performing yoga for vagus activation, try incorporating other techniques such as slow breathing, and meditation. To perform yoga well, you will need a quiet location with minimal disruptions. You will also need a yoga mat and a guide video. If you prefer performing among other individuals, you can get into a yoga studio around your home.

Tai-chi: Tai-chi is a form of wrestling technique originating from ancient China. The technique today is performed as a form of exercise. Tai-chi mainly involves slow horizontal movements with the hands placed in front of the practitioner. This type of exercise has been found to be calming and very helpful to individuals who wish to stimulate their vagus nerve. If you want to stimulate your vagus nerve, simply focus on working out on the slow movements. You can use a guided video to perform tai-chi, or you may choose to visit a studio near you.

Meditation for Vagus Nerve Activation

Meditation is one of the most important ways of activating the vagus nerve. Meditation can be used by any person, even those who have not attended meditation classes. As compared to tai-chi and yoga, which seem to be complex, meditation is a simple approach.

Meditation simply involves visualization. The practitioner has to visualize a certain environment that promotes calmness. The main aim of meditation in this process is to calm down the sympathetic action and activate the parasympathetic action of the vagus nerve. If you are capable of sending a signal to the brain that will initiate the actions of the parasympathetic nervous system, you will be in the right position to move on with your life.

To benefit from meditation, you need to choose the right type of meditation. There are many types of meditation. However, only a few are effective in calming down nerves and boosting your vagus nerve action. Some of the meditation techniques used to activate the vagus nerve include:

Mindfulness Meditation: In this type of meditation, the aim is to distract the mind from the thoughts that cause anxiety. When you practice mindfulness meditation, the focus is on yourself. You only think about yourself, your body, your environment, among others. If you want to enjoy the fruits of mindful meditation, you need to observe the rules for mindful meditation. First, during mindfulness, a person may discover some frustrating facts about themselves. In mindful meditation, you allow yourself to visualize yourself in a way that you have never done before. Therefore, all the benefits of the meditation should be protected by following the rules. One of the most important rules of this type of meditation is being non-judgmental. In other words, you are not allowed to judge yourself after observing your thoughts or feelings. You are required to embrace the truth about yourself. This action in itself promotes calming of nerves. Some people who suffer from depression only experience nervousness due to fear of being judged. However, if you can learn to accept your flaws through mindfulness meditation, you will not be shaken by anything. Mindfulness meditation teaches you to stand strong and believe in yourself no matter what the world may say about you. This is the attitude you need to overcome anxiety and depression. This attitude also promotes the parasympathetic activities of the vagus nerve.

Focused Meditation: Focused meditation is a type of meditation where the practitioner focuses their thoughts on a single object. In this type of meditation, you can choose any object in a room and simply focus on it. Focused meditation needs intense concentration. For instance, you can choose to focus on a chair or a wall. When performing focused meditation, you can't release your eyes from that piece of furniture. Use your mind to describe the chair and try looking at it based on different aspects. Think about its design, colors, shape, make, or any other aspect of the seat. Think about factors that make it special, how it holds weight, among others. This type of meditation is only intended to help you reduce the tension in your mind. After reducing the tension in your mind, the body can slowly reduce the sympathetic actions that are leading to anxiety.

Peace, Love, and Kindness Meditation: This is the most ideal type of meditation for individuals looking to activate the vagus nerve. The fact that a person may be experiencing anxiety or depression means that they need an activity that will lead to the calming down of nerves. There is no better activity than peace, love, and kindness meditation.

In this type of meditation, you have to visualize yourself as a center of peace, love, and kindness to the world. In your mind, you have to visualize a world without violence or hatred. In this world, you are the main source of peace, love, and kindness. In this type of meditation, you visualize yourself extending kindness to people who need it. You stand out as an individual who embraces those who are weak. In your routines, you provide peace and kindness to people who are close to you and try to show them that the world can be a better place. You freely give to people who need help on the streets. You may also visit your enemies and extend a hand of forgiveness. Create a perfect world in your visualization and just indulge in that peaceful world for a few minutes. When you are done with your meditation, you will be in the right place to let go of all your fears and anxiety. This calming effect activates the vagus nerve, allowing you to live a normal life again.

Simple Step By Step Guide To Meditation

Step1: Prepare the Meditation Room and Tools

For meditation to be successful, you must find a quiet location without interruptions. You can meditate in your bedroom or in an open space. It is important that the meditation location has plenty of fresh air and that it allows you to enjoy peace during meditation. You will also need a meditation mat or a right-back chair. You may need some meditation music, but it is not compulsory.

Step 2: Position Yourself for Meditation

Before you start your meditation, ensure that you have enough time to complete the session. Switch off all interruptions such as your cell phone and only use your watch to set a reminder for timing purposes. Position yourself on the mat in a sitting posture with your legs right in front. Sit in an upright position and allow yourself to freely breathe in the fresh air. If you are using a chair, ensure your back is aligned parallel to the straight back of the chair. This allows your back to be in an upright position, which is perfect for free breathing.

Step 3: Close Your Eyes and Focus on Your Breath

To prepare your mind for meditation, you need to draw your concentration. The easiest way to start concentrating is by focusing on your breathing for about 5 minutes. Do not try controlling how you breathe. Just focus your thoughts on it and feel how the air goes in and comes out. This will raise your awareness of the environment and will allow you to concentrate on the moment.

Step 4: Get into Visualization

Once your mind has been prepared for the process, get deep into visualization. With any type of meditation, you can follow this process. You only start by preparing your room, position yourself, and prepare your mind. Once you are ready, you can now focus your mind on whatever it is that the meditation technique requires. For instance, in focused meditation, you may now open your eyes and choose to focus on the ceiling in the room. If you know that you will be performing focused meditation, ensure that there is something you can focus on in the room. Interestingly, you cannot lack something to look at and try to describe in your own understanding. If you are performing peace, love, and kindness meditation, you have to close your eyes and create the images in your head. You have to start visualizing your activities as the ambassador for peace to those who need it. It is much simpler if you close your eyes and only focus on the meditation for a given period of time.

Natural Ways Of Vagus Nerve Stimulation

Besides meditation, slow breathing, and yoga, there are other techniques of vagus nerve stimulation that are less harmful. Look at these techniques and use them to stimulate your vagus nerve when you are anxious or nervous.

Chewing Gum: Chewing gum leads to the secretion of CCK, a gut hormone that directly activates vagal impulses. This explains why people are likely to remain active for long hours while chewing gum. When a person chews gum, he/she can go for hours without taking food. This is due to the vagal impulses that CCK sends to the brain. The brain is tricked into thinking that the person is eating food. This trick can be used to reduce the sensory actions that lead to feelings of hunger in a person.

Eat High Fiber Foods: High fiber foods have also been found to be helpful in stimulating the action of the vagus nerve. Fiber foods are a good source of GLP-1, a satiating hormone that is responsible for the stimulating vagus impulses in the brain. This hormone helps slow down gut action and as a result, makes a person feel fuller for a long time. Some of the important high fiber foods include grains such as barley and peas. You can also rely on carrots, nuts, and potatoes, among others.

Tai Chi: We have already looked at tai-chi as one of the most effective ways of stimulating the vagus nerve. This is a 100% natural process since it does not involve the use of electronic gadgets. Tai-chi is known for its ability to increase heart rate variability; as a result, directly influencing the actions of the vagus nerve.

Gargling: Gargling may seem like child's play to many, but it is an important exercise that may influence your vagus nerve health. Gargling activates the vagus nerve and stimulates the gastrointestinal tract. Naturally, it is the vagus nerve that is supposed to activate the muscles behind the throat, allowing you to gargle. However, in a case where the action of the vagus nerve is slow, and the body needs some stimulation, self-induced gargling leads to the contraction of the muscles in the back of your throat, hence stimulating the vagus nerve. You can naturally stimulate your vagus nerve by gargling water before you swallow it.

Singing or Chanting: Another way of influencing the activity of your vagus nerve is through singing and chanting. Singing increases heart variability, just like it is the case with tai chi. Some of the best chants and songs include humming, mantra recitation, hymn singing, etc. These types of songs or any hyperactivity dance and song performance can influence your vagus nerve to a large extent. When you sing, you stimulate the vagus pump, which sends relaxing waves to the brain through the choir. If you chant or sing at the top of your voice, you activate the muscles behind the throat, which stimulate the vagus nerve for action.

Positive Socialization: Social relationships can make a person overcome some of the negative emotions that lead to anxiety. If you relate well with people, you are more likely to feel calm and relaxed even when the situations are tough. In one study conducted by the Michigan University Psychology Department, participants were asked to sit separately and think compassionately about their family and friends. The participants were also required to silently repeat passionate phrases such as

........may you feel happy, may you feel safe, may you live well, etc.

Compared to those controlling the research, the participants of the exercise showed an overall increase in positive emotions such as joy, amusement, serenity, interest, among others. These changes were associated with a sense of being connected. As a result, the participants experienced improved vagal activity as observed through their heart rate variability. If you want to be genuinely happy and live well in all situations, you must learn to embrace people. Bring people together and love your life with joy.

Laughter: They say laughter is the best medicine. When it comes to taking care of your mental and social health, there is no better option than laughter. Several studies indicate that laughter is the best medicine since it stimulates the vagus nerve. One research showed that yoga laughter led to increased heart rate variability among the participants. This goes to show that the heart can be affected by your laughter. When a person laughs, the back muscles of the thought are stimulated in the same way as gargling. This stimulation leads to the activation of the vagus nerve, bringing in a feel-good sense. You can improve your vagus nerve health by getting involved in activities that promote laughter.

Chapter 14 Using Certain Equipment

In addition to all the active exercises that you can perform on your own, there are passive treatments that can have profound effects on the activation of the vagus nerve. Some of these involve using certain equipment or visiting a health care provider, while others you can do in the comfort of your own home.

Auricular Acupuncture

Acupuncture is an effective form of therapy for many conditions, and we have seen its spectacular effects firsthand using it with many patients as a hands-on chiropractor. If you recall, one of the four types of signals that vagus controls is sensation to specific parts of the external ear, or auricle: the entire concha, the crus of the helix, and the tragus. As such, stimulation of these specific regions will have effects that can stimulate the function of the vagus nerve.

The vagus nerve receives purely sensory information through its auricular branch via the central and anterior part of the ear. By using acupuncture, we can increase the flow of information in the auricular branch of VN, and thus increase VN activation. A significant and growing body of research shows that acupuncture and transcutaneous vagus nerve stimulation through the auricular branch of the VN yields positive effects in many patients suffering from depression, anxiety, epilepsy, LPS-induced inflammation, tinnitus, and highly active pain receptors.

Massage Therapy And Reflexology:

This feeling can be the epitome of parasympathetic activation and sympathetic deactivation. Not surprisingly, many different techniques of massage have been linked to increases in HRV levels or improved vagal tone including Chinese head massage; traditional Thai shoulder, neck, and head massage; traditional back massage; and even self-massage.

Visceral Manipulation:

Visceral manipulation (VM) is a less common therapy but one that is very effective when practiced correctly. Typically practiced by osteopaths, chiropractors, naturopaths, and other health care providers, VM is the gentle physical manipulation of the organs of the abdomen, thus increasing blood flow to areas that are not functioning optimally. Patients can use this feedback tool on their own, if learned correctly. As we know, the vagus nerve innervates all of the abdominal organs including the liver, gallbladder, pancreas, kidneys, spleen, stomach, small intestine, and ascending and transverse parts of the large intestine. For theVN to affect these organs and signal the brain about organ function, it is imperative that the organs function optimally. Physical restrictions can buildup in these organs that can only be altered by physical manipulation and mobilization. Improving blood flow to these organs can have significant beneficial results on organ health and allow the VN to send signals relating to optimal function.

Visceral manipulation therapist's use gently applied hands-on therapy to find areas of altered or decreased motion within the viscera and release restrictions within these visceral organs. The treatment involves a gentle compression, mobilization, or elongation of the soft tissues. Finding a certified visceral manipulation therapist in your area may be a good idea, especially for those people dealing with dysfunction with detoxification or with liver, gallbladder, or kidney pain.

Chiropractic Care:

Mechanical joint pain caused by lack of motion is more common than pain from overuse of a joint. In patients with neck pain, spinal manipulation performed by a chiropractor led to significant positive changes in blood pressure and heart rate variability, significantly improving VN activity. The reduction in pain levels allowed patients to breathe slower and improve their vagus nerve function, and that chiropractic manipulation provided a positive effect on patients' mechanical function. Especially when one is in pain, chiropractic care can be a very effective method of therapy and can have a significant benefit for VN and parasympathetic activity.

Electrical Stimulation:

This unit issued to treat patients dealing with severe treatment-resistant depression and/or epilepsy. Right-side VNS is effective in animal models of epilepsy and seizures, but is not known to have strong effects on depressive symptoms. Preliminary human trials are promising and have yielded positive effects, and some companies have already begun creating vagus nerve stimulation tools that can be used for various conditions. The Cardio Fit system from Bio Control Medical uses right-side VNS to activate efferent fibers and aid in treatment of heart failure, while the Fitness System from Bio Control Medical is designed to activate afferent fibers, thus helping to reduce side effects of electrical vagal stimulation. There are other devices for electrical stimulation that do not need to be implanted, though they show mixed results and are approved for certain conditions only at this point. As we well know, the body has a strong anti-inflammatory system, and if the VN is exercised and functioning correctly, this system can improve overall health significantly by keeping inflammation levels in check.

Enemas

When you think of stimulating the vagus nerve, enemas probably aren't the first thing that comes to mind, but they can be very effective. After all, the vagus nerve is particularly affected by the gut and so if you activate it, you activate the vagus nerve.

When you insert liquid into the rectum, your body must hold it in. This exerts control over your body and activates the pelvis, which also activates the vagus nerve. Resisting the urge to defecate is actually very helpful in toning the vagus nerve, so enemas can be useful for this purpose, but the type of enema is also important.

Coffee can be used to give yourself an enema that will stimulate the vagus nerve. Any liquid will help with this, but coffee is best, because it contains compounds that actually stimulate nerve endings. In addition, it gets the bile ducts flowing, which helps with digestion.

Enemas in general, as well as those with coffee, help flush toxins out of the bowels, too. This reduces inflammation and helps improve vagal tone. You can make your own enema from cool coffee, or you can buy pre-made enemas in bottles that are easily used. If you make your own, stick to one teaspoon of coffee grounds per enema, as it can be too strong to use full coffee.

Acupressure And Acupuncture

Acupuncture and acupressure are very similar, apart from the fact that one uses pressure and the other uses very thin needles to stimulate specific pressure points. Both methods allow you to physically stimulate the vagus nerve and enhance the parasympathetic reaction. It's considered a good alternative to the implant that we looked at.

By inserting needles or adding pressure to specific points in the body, it's possible to stimulate the vagus nerve and rapidly improve its tone. This is something you can do at any practitioner's office and they should be well aware of which points to use in order to open up the nerve's function.

5 Powerful Tips For Handling Workers And Anxiety

Do you feel you can go crazy if you continue working in such a stressful place? Most people who work in stressful situations feel this way from time to time. You are not unique in your feelings.

It is imperative to discover how to address the concern in the workplace. Excessive stress and anxiety can negatively affect your production and health. Learning to deal with stress can make the difference between being promoted and looking for a new job.

THE Techniques to deal with stress at work.

When you are under pressure at work, you need to learn what is called "government control."

The "state" in "state control" refers to your emotional state. There are several ways to control your emotional state.

Here are five work stress techniques:

1. The first technique that feels that your blood starts to boil is breathing. Correct, simple breathing activates the so-called vagus nerve. The vagus nerve, in turn, enables the relaxation of chemicals that are released in the brain and soothe it immediately.

2. Write a list of tasks. Writing a list of all the required activities will help clear your mind. Almost like the circus artist who balances numerous turntables, his subconscious does the same

and continually reminds him of all the things he doesn't want to forget. Writing down tasks allows you to leave a turntable.

3. Have a fun plan. If you have nothing to expect, work can become too stressful to deal with quickly. A good weekend or participating in your favorite hobby or sport can make stress much more bearable.

4. Try to anchor. Is there a specific aroma that will take you to a calm and happy moment? Maybe the scent of the nails takes you to a relaxed Christmas scene. Or perhaps the image of the ocean will help you imagine being on the beach. An anchor is all that helps change your emotional state.

5. Listen to harmonic music. It has been shown that harmonious music, such as classical music, helps to relax and slow down neurons in the brain to reduce stress effectively. An additional benefit is to think better, which leads to better productivity.

Everyday work stress is increasing. Take action today to avoid problems that may arise tomorrow.

These techniques are powerful, but not enough. There are more techniques to relieve the stress you need to acquire to alleviate your stress and anxiety. Discover how you can permanently ease stress and anxiety in just a few minutes.

Chapter 15 Chew and Whistle, A Medicinal Product That Can Work In Cold And Common Breast Bronchitis

Most people suffer from a disease that causes coughing and wheezing, and no one has been immune to the devastation of floating viruses that are transmitted from person to person and affect human existence. A gasp of unbearable mucus, which adheres to the air intake ducts of the lungs and makes noises that drive everyone crazy, always remains present without the extraction being supported by an external source.

Cough and wheezing can be caused by many different diseases associated with diseases that produce increasing mucus from the lungs or narrow ducts that represent the absorption of oxygen in the body to keep it alive.

There are a minimum of 17 conditions that can cause wheezing. Most coughs are caused by conditions that can cause wheezing since, in most cases, the mucus has to be expelled, and the mucus gets stuck in the airways that cause wheezing.

In cases of a breast infection, commonly known as "breast cancer," in which cold is absorbed and remains in a person's lungs, the lungs can produce mucus all the time and endlessly. Chop and cough a large amount of mucus and five minutes cough more. This cycle of drool and cough never seems to end, while the whistle, which sounds like a musical instrument, plays the same note for you all day and all night.

One of the most common causes of cough and excessive wheezing, along with the cold virus, is bronchitis. Millions of people have this supply, which narrows the airways in their lungs due to supposed cramping. Very often, bronchitis becomes inflamed with the fall in winter temperatures. I could call this a problem of the vagus nerve because the capillaries of the body expand and contract with the outside temperature to cool and heat the internal organs of the body. Doctors refer to a narrowing of the pulmonary airways as a "cramp" when contraction occurs, but in speculation, can the vagus nerve play a role in bronchial cramps?

Cough syrup has been formulated to dilute and loosen mucus during a so-called bronchial spasm so that the mucus can pass through narrow ducts. When the mucus comes from a common cold, it is speculated that a constant flow of mucus will be created to eliminate the cold sinus virus.

Asthma and pneumonia are two different stories of what I am talking about in this article. Cancer can also cause wheezing, and you should consult a doctor if you do not know if your wheezing and coughing are due to bronchitis or the common cold virus.

My last cold the last time I suffered from wheezing was included for the first time, and it was not an easy task to find a cure for wheezing. Thanks to the Internet, I was able to find a tool that would help me, and, to my surprise, what I found worked. I have read many websites that have written about coughing and wheezing, including sites with natural remedies.

What I found useful is "Ibuprofen," "Coffee with caffeine," and a "Portable floor heater." I found the drug "Ibuprofen" on a medical website, the drug "Coffee" on a natural remedies website, and I came up with the idea of using the floor heater of another natural remedies website that uses steam from a shower of hot water. Dissolves mucus in a person's lungs.

Most of the things that were mentioned on the natural remedies websites were inconvenient in terms of the time they would take and would not work as well as I would have liked a home remedy. All things on medical websites were medications and surgery, and avoiding the doctor is the game plan.

I tried "ibuprofen" and immediately noticed results. "Caffeinated coffee" helps, but it is one of those remedies that won't last long unless you drink coffee all day. I drink coffee anyway, who cares! Help some. I read that in the days of old coffee, the best cure was cough and wheezing.

A "floor heater" is what works, and it seems that it will restore the airways in a person's lungs for 4 to 6 hours and slow mucus production. I read about the hot shower and the steam and tried without lasting results. I decided to take out my underfloor heating and inhale the warm air and "BINGO!" I came to the jackpot, got rid of the wheezing, and stopped the cough until I could sleep and function normally for about 6 hours.

I used the three remedies. The three work well together. However, ibuprofen should only be used at night. Take only two tablets a day because overdoing over-the-counter pain relievers is terrible for the liver. You can use underfloor heating or even a hairdryer all day — a car heater to go to. Just don't get too close and don't breathe scorching air. Otherwise, you could burn your lungs. I found 5 to 10 minutes away 12 to 15 inches apart, and I will do the trick. Breathe deeply so that the hot air fills all the ducts of the lungs. After that, mucus may appear for 30 to 60 minutes. However, this is only your lungs, which Eliminates the existing mucus. There may also be a very low whistle, but it won't be unfortunate enough to drive you crazy.

This method of treating cough and wheezing is my own experience that works for me. If you have any questions, always consult a doctor and use "Never" over-the-counter pain relievers as a panacea. Never inhale scorching air! Set a certain distance between the heater and your face.

Chapter 16 Can Vagus Nerve Stimulation Treat Heart Diseases?

This research is based on facts, for example, we know that the autonomic nervous system is unbalanced in patients with heart failure, that the sympathetic nerves are overexcited and the parasympathetic nerves are suppressed; we know that ACEI, ARBs, BBs, aldosterone receptor antagonists and similar methods can regulate the sympathetic nerve's excessive excitement and improved clinical outcomes; we understand that stimulation of the vagus nerve can monitor sympathetic nerve activity through two sites, presynaptic (adrenaline release) and postsynaptic (cell). Finally, from animal experiments, we know that vagal and spinal cord stimulation can regulate sympathetic nerve activity to improve the prognosis of heart failure, including reversal of left ventricular remodeling in animals and improvement of prognosis in patients with non-control clinical research center failure.

The above existing knowledge inevitably leads to the hypothesis that vagal nerve stimulation is beneficial for regulating the sympathetic innervation to improve the prognosis of patients with heart failure. It is suggested that patients in the control group should implant an object that has not been activated, but it will not affect the time to the primary endpoint of "hospitalization or all-cause death due to unplanned heart failure or lack of changing ultrasound measurements value. However, there may be some placebo effects in this study. These effects will affect the improvement of NYHA cardiac function grade, six-minute walking distance, and quality of life. We must also consider whether the dose, location, and type of vagus nerve stimulation are wrong. The cervical vagus nerve contains sympathetic nerve fibers that can be activated to excite the stellate ganglia, so cervical vagus nerve stimulation is a stimulation of the vagus sympathetic trunk. Second, as in a recent study in dogs, cervical vagus nerve stimulation can also damage sympathetic ganglia, but the effect is unknown.

Prevent Ageing By Stimulating The Vagus Nerve In The Ear

Stimulation of the vagus nerve via the outer ear can inhibit the aging of the body through a partial revitalization of the nervous system. The research was conducted among 29 healthy people aged at least 55 years. An apparatus stimulating the vagus nerve, belonging to the autonomic nervous system, was connected to their outer ear.

The vagus nerve is the longest cranial and mixed nerve, whose fibers leave the brain to many parts of the body and organs, including the muscles of the throat, larynx, and palate, heart, lungs, intestines, and kidney. One of them also reaches the outer ear. The vagus nerve affects the functioning of many systems, regulates lung function, heart and blood pressure as well as the digestive system. With age, the human nervous system is less functional, which affects the entire body. The vagus nerve also functions worse.

The research focused on stimulating this nerve via an apparatus connected to the outer ear. This stimulation ensures - is painless; only gentle tickling can be felt. During tests, it was performed for 15 minutes, a day over two weeks, the research specialist claims that after such simple procedures, the examined volunteers improved the balance between the sympathetic (stimulating) and parasympathetic (inhibitory) system; this was most evident in people in whom it was most disturbed; this meant that their well-being improved more clearly, such people also slept better. The research specialist admits that observations are needed for a larger group of people over the longer term. However, the results obtained are only the "tip of the iceberg" of what can be achieved by vagus nerve stimulation. Further attempts are to show, for example, whether this method will enable the treatment of heart failure, depression, and irritable bowel syndrome.

Intestinal Brain And Health Effect

The brain affects the health of the intestine, and the intestine, in turn, affects the health of the brain.

Surprisingly, however, we notice that the intestine is the main reason for this communication. Only 10% of this communication information is transmitted from the brain to the intestine, while 90% is the intestine that speaks to the brain! Nutrition, immune system, and intestinal flora have direct effects on brain health, and it affects our emotions and mental health.

You will surely know at least one person in your environment who is experiencing mood swings, phobias, depression or Alzheimer's, or some other Neurodegenerative disease that has its cause in the brain and nervous system. The communication between these two vital organs, our two brains, is by no means accidental.

As has already been shown in the womb, during pregnancy, these two organs are formed by the same tissue. So even in adulthood, there is direct communication between them, which is the gut.

Communication occurs in many different ways. In principle, part of the interface follows the path of the spinal nervous system. Another significant part follows the pulmonary gastric nerve (to which a particular article will be devoted hereafter), which is a large nerve that connects the brainstem with the digestive system. Another way of communication is the intestinal nervous system, which has 100 million nerve cells along the intestinal tract and is an autonomic nervous system that also communicates with the brain.

Also, these various neural pathways of communication are the intestinal flora bacteria that contribute to communication, which do not seem to have the exclusive occupation of digesting food. These bacteria secrete various transmitter substances to communicate with each other and with the rest of the body. Also, they have specific receptors (proteins) that attach to the brain via the nerves.

Basic Exercise

Here is a first practice exercise that helps to restore the "social nervous system" as it restores the atlas and 2nd vertebra to their right position and allows for greater flexibility in the movement of the neck and the entire spine.

Through this restoration to the correct position, the brain base is enlarged, from where the five underlying brain nerves originate or exit, which positively affects both the anterior branch of the lung and the nerves V, VII, IX, and XI.

Before exercising, check for free movement of the neck by trying to turn your head as far as you can to the left and right. Observe if you have pain, discomfort, or some grip.

After exercising, recheck the freedom of movement; if It has improved; usually, the first application dramatically improves the range of motion of the neck. The first few times, it is best to run it sideways. It can be performed in an upright or sitting position.

☐ Cross your fingertips at the back of your head

☐ Place your arms crossed at the base of your head, allowing the weight of the head to rest comfortably on your crossed fingers. If you have a grip that prevents movement with both hands, try one hand under the head at the same time.

☐ do not shake your head. Turn your eyes only to one side, e.g., to the right and hold this eye position for 30 to 60 seconds. Wait for this position until there is a mood for yawning, drowsiness, or swallowing; this is the slogan that the autonomic nervous system has relaxed.

☐ Turn your eyes now in the center and then look at the opposite side, e.g., left.

☐ Hold this position again without shaking your head until you have a mood for yawning, shivering, or swallowing.

☐ by completing this cycle, you have already completed the necessary exercise. Take your hands off your head and recover. If you feel dizzy, do not worry that it will take 2 minutes. Your pressure has dropped from relaxation.

Observe the range of freedom of movement of your neck again. Change something; did you notice a change in mood and energy that floods your brain?

Vagus Nerve Stimulation for Epilepsy

If epilepsy cannot be managed with medication, then surgery, a ketogenic diet, or vagus nerve stimulation must be considered. One of the relatively "young" methods of treating drug-resistant epilepsy is vagus nerve stimulation (VNS). The vagus nerve has a specific structure; this is the X cranial nerve, guiding motor and parasympathetic fibers; the nuclei of this nerve area in the brain. The vagus nerve itself is very long and innervates several regions of the body, including the neck, chest, and abdominal organs. The mechanism of antiepileptic action of vagus nerve stimulation has not yet been thoroughly understood, although it is believed that it is the effect of stimulation on the nerve pathways to the noradrenergic and serotonergic systems.

VNS is a therapy based on irritating the left vagus nerve.

The stimulator is powered by a battery with a lifetime of about ten years. The device is equipped with a power generator, which leads to the vagus nerve. Thanks to the radio system, it is possible to control the pacemaker, e.g., you can change parameters and turn off the device.

Indication for treatment is epilepsy resistant to pharmacological polytherapy in people over 12 years of age, as well as drug-resistant chronic and recurrent depression. The use of VNS in other mental illnesses has not yet been analyzed.

What Is The Nature Of The Treatment?

To start treatment through VNS, it is necessary to undergo surgery to implant the pacemaker. The patient is under general anesthesia. The stimulator is usually implanted under the skin on the chest. Then, from the pacemaker, special electrodes need to be made around the neck that will transmit electrical impulses to the vagus nerve. After the implantation, the operating doctor always performs a pacemaker fitness test.

Then the device is programmed by the attending physician in the homeward. The stimulator begins to generate

Cyclical electrical impulses in series lasting half a minute, alternating with 5-minute breaks, at a specified intensity and frequency. It is also possible to set the "impulse on demand" by placing a magnet so that when you feel the aura, you can start stimulation and thus limit the occurrence of an epileptic seizure. VNS therapy can last for several months to several years. The patient is then subject to regular, monthly, or even more frequent checks at the attending physician.

It is worth knowing that a transdermal stimulator is also available "on the market." Using it does not require surgery. It consists of stimulating the branch of the vagus nerve in the ear region through the rear electrode.

Efficacy of Vagus Nerve Stimulation for Epilepsy The effectiveness of VNS in the treatment of epilepsy is similar to that of new-generation antiepileptic drugs.

Seizures after implanting the pacemaker may disappear even in a dozen or so percent of patients, and in about 50-60% be halved. The effectiveness of treatment in drug-resistant depression is not yet as well documented as in epilepsy. However, there has been an improvement in the condition of depressed patients undergoing VNS. The method seems to be more effective in milder depression, which responds to drugs only to a small extent. It is essential to know that there is not always an improvement in the treatment of drug-resistant depression. Also, the patient's mental state deteriorates extremely rarely (transition to the manic phase, one case of suicide).

Cons of VNS for epilepsy

The disadvantage of vagus nerve stimulation is the appearance of local complaints related to the pacemaker.

They are generally mild and transient:

☐ Neck pain and paresthesia

☐ Voice change and hoarseness

☐ Larynx cramps, nausea

☐ Headaches,

☐ Cough, swallowing, and breath problems during stimulation.

It should also be remembered that patients with an implanted vagus nerve cannot have magnetic resonance imaging.

Conclusion

If I had told you at the start that there is one nerve in the body whose activity effectively controls our destinies, perhaps you wouldn't have believed me. In fact, it would still be hard to believe up until now, if not for the wealth of scientific resources one can find about this topic. There is a huge body of research on disparate topics, all joined together only by the fact that the vagus nerve has something to do with them.

Perhaps it's a good time to really appreciate the wonder and complexity of the human body. Many of us had been taught of the body as a sort of computer where the brain is the central processing unit, the heart is the battery, and the lungs and gut the power cords connecting us to the power supply that is food, water, and air. But the human body is instead an intricate and highly organic system, where even the mighty brain takes cues from the rest of the body. Every organ system has a hand in determining the steps for the body, and somewhere in that great switchboard of information, the vagus nerve sits trying to sort everything out.

This has taken you through the whole gamut of research and details on the vagus nerve. By now, you should know pretty much everything there is to know about it, from its anatomy to its myriad of functions, from harnessing it for overall health to the issues that it can address in the near future.

But if there is one piece of info that you should never forget out of all that you have read, it is this: the vagus nerve is just a part of a network, a vast network of feedback and control, of input and assessment that we have not yet completely explored and mapped. With all this information on the vagus nerve, it would be so easy to spend all your time trying to stimulate your vagus nerve to its optimal tone. Now, all that's good, but it's still just a part of the overall equation of health.

Remember that the vagus nerve does not just relay information from the brain to the rest of the body. It also actively picks up information from the rest of the body, sending it up to the brain. While one can (in the light of all the research we covered) make the assertion that a person can only be as healthy as his vagus nerve, it would be more accurate to say that the vagus nerve could only be as healthy as the organ surrounding it.

You could have a perfectly functioning active vagus nerve... but you may still develop various illnesses thanks to your lifestyle choices. You may still be a victim of one of the GBDs. Note that while vagus stimulation can ward off certain issues, the vagus nerve is more or less just a mirror reflecting your state of overall health when it comes to other illnesses. It's so easy to confuse these two concepts. Stimulating your vagus nerve can't (at least not yet) cure cancer, but this cancer can show important signs when viewed through the vagus nerve.

In short, take care of the vagus nerve as much as you need — do the "bullet time" breathing exercises (or take a deep look at the contemplative traditions if you have time), fix your diet, do a routine vagal massage, and perk up your posture. But don't neglect the rest of the body, too. When you feel that something is wrong with a different part of the body, seek ways to cure it independently of vagus stimulation — but let the stimulation continue as a means of augmenting whatever other remedy you may use.

Observing the vagus nerve up close shows us a very important lesson, too. We are exposed to the idea that what we know about the slew of diseases affecting the world might just be the tip of the iceberg. With all the in-depth research we have, we are just gradually becoming more and more aware of just how interconnected things are, and how seemingly disparate things can actually be deeply related because of an overarching factor. Who knew that a reading in the EEG could predict whether or not you are likely to suffer from depression? Who knew that stimulating something other than the brain could help the brain repair itself from stroke? Who knew that the word "gut feel" actually has scientific backing, since the gut indeed talks to the brain? Who knew that the microbial flora in one's gut could even affect how moody a person can be?

One can only imagine the surprise of the first people who discovered the wonders of the vagus nerve. Today, that wonder lives on in the people who have had the opportunity to explore the powers of this twin bundle of nerve fibers winding its way through the human body. Just do a cursory search online and you will be seeing a lot of articles hailing the vagus nerve as the body's best kept secret to health, a holy grail of cures.

But again, be careful of such labeling. The vagus nerve isn't the Holy Grail — the human body, as a whole, is. We haven't even mapped the entirety of the vagus nerve yet, and science is still busy trying to find the best way to tame and stimulate it. But who knows if, in the future, we find some specific part of the vagus nerve — or a different part of the body, for that matter — that will concentrate all the nerve's powers into a smaller area? And then another one before that? The search for "the secret" will always continue, but never take your eyes off the fact that the body is a holistic system, meant to function as a whole.

Just like the meditative masters of old, may the knowledge you gained about the vagus nerve serve as building blocks on which you can build something synergistic — something that really is at one with the body and everything that is around it.

CPSIA information can be obtained
at www.ICGtesting.com
Printed in the USA
BVHW041350121120
593173BV00007B/154